AMERICA ★ THE ★ BEAUTIFUL

How to Use This Book

Look for these special features in this book:

SIDEBARS, **CHARTS**, **GRAPHS**, and original **MAPS** expand your understanding of what's being discussed—and also make useful sources for classroom reports.

FAQs answer common **F**requently **A**sked **Q**uestions about people, places, and things.

WOW FACTORS offer "Who knew?" facts to keep you thinking.

TRAVEL GUIDE gives you tips on exploring the state—either in person or right from your chair!

PROJECT ROOM provides fun ideas for school assignments and incredible research projects. Plus, there's a guide to primary sources—what they are and how to cite them.

Please note: All statistics are as up-to-date as possible at the time of publication.

Consultants: William Loren Katz; Barry S. Kues, Professor, Department of Earth and Planetary Science, University of New Mexico; Bárbara O. Reyes, Professor of History, University of New Mexico

Book production by The Design Lab

Library of Congress Cataloging-in-Publication Data
Burgan, Michael.
 New Mexico / by Michael Burgan.
   p. cm.—(America the beautiful. Third series)
 Includes bibliographical references.
 ISBN-13: 978-0-531-18578-0
 ISBN-10: 0-531-18578-8
 1. New Mexico—Juvenile literature. I. Title. II. Series.
 F796.3.B87 2008
 978.9—dc22   2007007728

BY MICHAEL BURGAN

Third Series

Children's Press®
An Imprint of Scholastic Inc.
New York ★ Toronto ★ London ★ Auckland ★ Sydney
Mexico City ★ New Delhi ★ Hong Kong
Danbury, Connecticut

CONTENTS

1 LAND

Millions of years ago, fiery volcanoes shaped the land. Today, the state is home to forest-dwelling owls and elk that roam mountainsides. . . . **8**

2 FIRST PEOPLE

The Anasazis built huge stone and mud-brick homes and learned to raise crops. Pueblos made pottery, and Navajos and Apaches arrived from the north. . . . **22**

3 EXPLORATION AND SETTLEMENT

Spanish explorers trekked north from Mexico, lured by dreams of gold. Instead, they found the Pueblo people, who sometimes resisted the newcomers. . . . **32**

6 PEOPLE

Spanish descendants, Native Americans, and Anglos shape New Mexico, as do people from other diverse backgrounds. . . . **64**

7 GOVERNMENT

State, county, and city officials make laws, while Native American nations have their own governments. **80**

8 ECONOMY

Tourism, the arts, space exploration—they all play a part in keeping New Mexicans working. **92**

GROWTH AND CHANGE 4

U.S. soldiers followed American traders into New Mexico, which in 1848 became part of the United States. And Native Americans soon lost their land. **42**

MORE MODERN TIMES

5

New Mexicans played vital roles in World War II, and the state became a center for high-tech research. **54**

9 TRAVEL GUIDE

Plunge deep into the earth or scale high peaks in a land filled with enchanting natural wonders and impressive historic sites. **102**

PROJECT ROOM

★

PROJECTS. 116

TIMELINE 122

GLOSSARY 125

FAST FACTS 126

BIOGRAPHICAL DICTIONARY. . .133

RESOURCES 137

★

INDEX 139

AUTHOR'S TIPS AND SOURCE NOTES 143

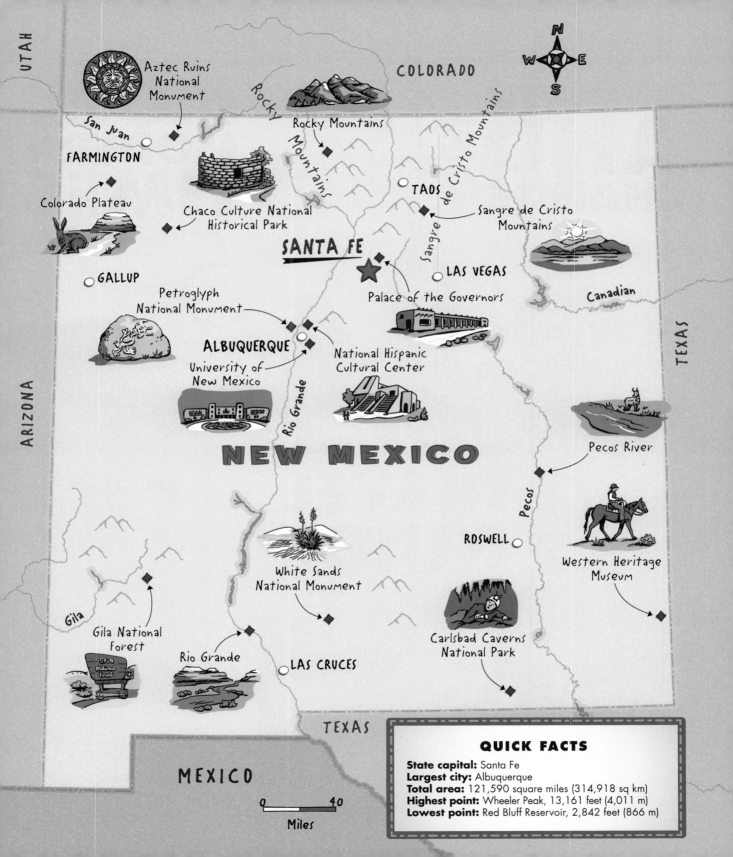

UTAH

COLORADO

Aztec Ruins
National
Monument

San Juan

Rocky
Mountains

Rocky Mountains

Sangre de Cristo Mountains

N
W E
S

FARMINGTON

Colorado Plateau

Chaco Culture National
Historical Park

TAOS

Sangre de Cristo
Mountains

SANTA FE

GALLUP

Petroglyph
National Monument

LAS VEGAS

Palace of the Governors

Canadian

ALBUQUERQUE

University of
New Mexico

National Hispanic
Cultural Center

ARIZONA

TEXAS

Rio Grande

NEW MEXICO

Pecos River

Pecos

Gila

Gila National
Forest

White Sands
National Monument

ROSWELL

Western Heritage
Museum

Rio Grande

LAS CRUCES

Carlsbad Caverns
National Park

TEXAS

MEXICO

0   40

Miles

QUICK FACTS

State capital: Santa Fe
Largest city: Albuquerque
Total area: 121,590 square miles (314,918 sq km)
Highest point: Wheeler Peak, 13,161 feet (4,011 m)
Lowest point: Red Bluff Reservoir, 2,842 feet (866 m)

Welcome to New Mexico!

HOW DID NEW MEXICO GET ITS NAME?

About 800 years ago, a people called the Mexicas settled in a valley south of what is now the United States. In time, the Mexicas became part of the great Aztec empire. The capital of this empire was called Mexico Tenochtitlan. The city was located on an island in waters called the Lake of the Moon. In the Aztec language, Mexico means "in the center of the moon." It referred to the location of the capital. Spain began conquering the Aztecs in 1519 and started calling the former Aztec lands Nueva España, or New Spain. But the capital city and nearby region were still sometimes called Mexico. Within several decades, Spanish explorers ventured north from New Spain. They found high desert land and called the area La Nueva Mexico—"the New Mexico." The name *New Mexico* reflects the three cultures—Native American, Hispanic, and English—that shape the state today.

8

READ ABOUT

New Mexico's
Ancient
Past 11

Land
Regions 13

Climate 17

Plant
Life 18

Animal
Life 20

Humans and the
Environment...21

The view along
Box Trail at Ghost
Ranch in Abiquiu

CHAPTER ONE

LAND

★

L ICENSE PLATES IN NEW MEXICO HAVE "U.S.A." AFTER THE STATE'S NAME. This is to remind everyone that New Mexico is part of the United States! With its 121,590 square miles (314,918 square kilometers), it is the nation's fifth-largest state. New Mexico has snowy peaks, high grassy plains, deep canyons, hot deserts, and forests filled with wildlife. From its highest point, Wheeler Peak at 13,161 feet (4,011 meters), to its lowest, Red Bluff Reservoir at 2,842 feet (866 m), its varied land helps explain the state's nickname—the Land of Enchantment.

New Mexico Topography

Use the color-coded elevation chart to see on the map New Mexico's high points (dark red to orange) and low points (green). Elevation is measured as the distance above or below sea level.

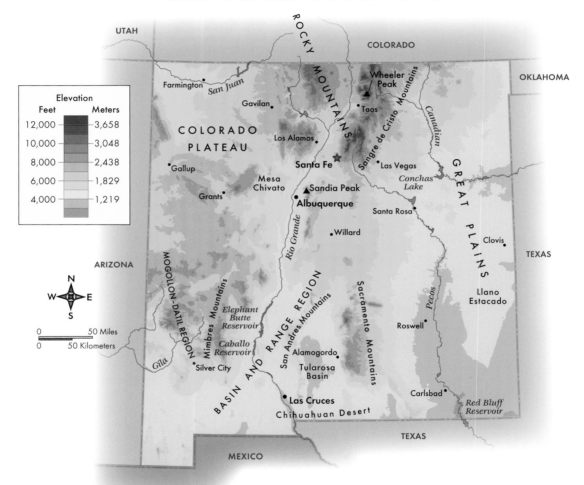

New Mexico's average elevation is about 4,700 feet (1,430 m) above sea level. That's almost a mile high!

HEART OF THE SOUTHWEST

New Mexico sits in the southwestern United States. It is almost a square, with each of its sides about 350 miles (550 km) long. It is bordered by five states: Arizona, Utah, Colorado, Oklahoma, and Texas. The country of Mexico stretches along its southwestern border.

New Mexico Geo-Facts

Along with the state's geographical highlights, this chart ranks New Mexico's land, water, and total area compared to all other states.

Total area; rank . . . . 121,590 square miles (314,918 sq km); 5th
Land; rank . . . . 121,356 square miles (314,310 sq km); 5th
Water; rank . . . . 234 square miles (606 sq km); 49th
Inland water; rank . . . . 234 square miles (606 sq km); 45th
Geographic center . . . . Torrance County, 12 miles (19 km)
southwest of Willard
Latitude . . . . 31°20' N to 37° N
Longitude . . . . 103° W to 109° W
Highest point . . . . Wheeler Peak, 13,161 feet (4,011 m)
Lowest point . . . . Red Bluff Reservoir, 2,842 feet (866 m)
Largest city . . . . Albuquerque
Longest river . . . . Rio Grande

Source: U.S. Census Bureau

WOW The state of Rhode Island could fit inside New Mexico 78 times!

NEW MEXICO'S ANCIENT PAST

Today, New Mexico is surrounded by land, and only a few major rivers cut across the state. But for most of the last 500 million years, New Mexico was covered by oceans. The last one disappeared from the region about 70 million years ago.

Fossils provide clues about the plants and animals that thrived millions of years ago. New Mexico's fossil record is one of the best and most complete in the United States. Fossil forests of **petrified** stumps and logs have been found in New Mexico, as have dinosaurs of all sorts and sizes. In the 1940s, hundreds of skeletons of a dinosaur called *Coelophysis* were found in northern New Mexico. It is now the state fossil.

WORDS TO KNOW

fossils *the remains or prints of ancient animals or plants left in stone*

petrified *changed into a stony hardness*

The Rio Grande Rift continues to widen from volcanic activity.

Seismosaurus ("earth shaker"), another dinosaur found in New Mexico, was among the largest of all dinosaurs, sometimes reaching more than 110 feet (34 m) long.

After the dinosaurs died out about 65 million years ago, the landscape continued to change. The Rio Grande Rift cuts through the central part of New Mexico. A rift is a split in the earth's outer layer, called the crust. About 29 million years ago, the land began to pull apart along the Rio Grande Rift. This motion created the mountains that now run from north to south through much of New Mexico. The Rio Grande later flowed through valleys created by the rift. Activity just below Earth's surface also led to the creation of many volcanoes in New Mexico. Capulin, in northeastern New Mexico, is the cone of a volcano that erupted about 60,000 years ago.

LAND REGIONS

New Mexico has five main land regions. In the east is the Great Plains. The north-central part of the state is dominated by the Rocky Mountains and smaller mountain chains. In the southwest is the rugged Mogollon-Datil region. The Rio Grande Rift and the southwestern part of the state are in the Basin and Range region. And the northwest corner of the state is part of the Colorado **Plateau**.

The Great Plains

The Great Plains stretches from Canada across the central United States and into Texas. The edge of this region touches eastern New Mexico. There the high, dry, flat land is called the Llano Estacado, which is Spanish for "palisaded plain." A palisade is a fence

WORD TO KNOW

plateau *an elevated part of the earth with steep slopes*

Storm clouds hang over the Llano Estacado.

A hiker stops to take a rest along the Pecos River.

made of wooden stakes. The name may refer to the steep mesas that rise around the plain. A 19th-century U.S. general called the Llano Estacado a "great North American desert." Although water is scarce, parts of the region are covered with grasslands that were once home to huge herds of bison. New Mexico's state grass, the blue grama, grows on the Llano Estacado.

The Pecos River marks the western edge of the Great Plains region. It then flows through southeastern New Mexico on its way to the Rio Grande. The Canadian River flows through the northern part of the Llano Estacado.

The Rocky Mountains

Some of the highest peaks in North America can be found in the Rocky Mountains. New Mexico is the home of the southern end of this mountain chain. Several smaller chains make up the Rockies in New Mexico. The tallest of these, the Sangre de Cristo Mountains, is in the north. The state's highest point, Wheeler Peak, is located near Taos in the Sangre de Cristos. The Rio Grande, New Mexico's longest river, cuts through the mountains. North of Taos, the river rolls along through a **gorge** that is 800 feet (244 m) deep.

The Mogollon-Datil Region

The Mogollon-Datil region lies in west-central and south-western New Mexico and extends into Arizona. Many rugged mountain ranges, mostly remnants of more than 20 gigantic collapsed volcanoes, dominate this region. The Gila Wilderness, one of New Mexico's least spoiled areas, lies in the Mogollon-Datil region.

The Basin and Range

Most of southern New Mexico and most of the Rio Grande Rift are part of a larger region of the western United States called the Basin and Range. In this region, narrow mountain ranges alternate with broad, flat areas called basins. In New Mexico, parts of the Sonoran and the Chihuahuan deserts lie in the southwest of this region. The Rio Grande runs along the Rio Grande Rift in the Basin and Range as it heads south. Eventually, the river becomes the border between the United States and Mexico.

WORD TO KNOW

gorge *a narrow, steep-walled canyon*

SEE IT HERE!

CARLSBAD CAVERNS NATIONAL PARK

Carlsbad Caverns, New Mexico's only national park, lies under the Chihuahuan Desert in the Guadalupe Mountains. More than 100 of the caverns in its vast underground cave system have been explored. Another 200 have yet to be explored. A half million people go to the park every year to visit giant caverns filled with wild rock formations. Those that hang from the ceiling are called stalactites. Pillars that grow up from the floor of the caverns are called stalagmites. Carlsbad Caverns is also home to hundreds of thousands of Mexican free-tailed bats. Each night, from spring until fall, they leave the caves by the thousands to hunt for their dinner—insects!

MINI-BIO

JIM WHITE: CARLSBAD'S "CAVE MAN"

Native Americans knew about the Carlsbad Caverns more than a thousand years ago. Early European settlers in the region also knew about the caves. But Jim White (1882–1946), a New Mexico cowboy, is given credit for exploring the cave system and telling the world about it. White was born in Texas, but moved to New Mexico as a boy. Seeing large waves of bats flying out of a big hole led him to the caves. He later wrote, "Any hole in the ground which could house such a gigantic army of bats must be a whale of a big cave." Using ropes and simple lanterns, he and a young assistant began to explore the caves. In the years to come, White built trails in the caves and led visitors on tours. His efforts led the U.S. government to name Carlsbad Caverns a national monument in 1923. Seven years later, it became a national park.

? Want to know more? See www.pbs.org/weekend explorer/newmexico/carlsbad/carlsbad_white.htm

Two of the larger mountain ranges in the Basin and Range are the Sacramento and the San Andres. Between them is the Tularosa Basin, the home of White Sands National Monument. Here, tall dunes of white sand stretch in every direction. The sand is actually a mineral called gypsum, which was left behind after a lake that covered most of the basin dried up about 12,000 years ago.

A boy runs through the dunes at White Sands National Monument.

The Colorado Plateau

The Colorado Plateau covers several states, including the northwestern part of New Mexico. Here you'll find the state's "badlands," stretches of high desert where few plants grow. The badlands is an area of large rocks shaped by **erosion**. Some of these rocks look like they belong on another planet, and many are filled with dinosaur bones, petrified logs, and other fossils. Erosion has also sculpted the remains of ancient volcanoes. El Malpais National Monument is near Grants, in western New Mexico. *Malpais* is Spanish for "badlands," and the main attraction here is hardened lava beds, the result of an eruption about 3,500 years ago.

CLIMATE

New Mexico is generally dry and sunny. But within this sunny land, rain and snow fall in the northern parts of the state. The driest parts of New Mexico are the deserts and **semiarid** regions of the south and west. These are also the state's hottest areas. Las Cruces, in the south, has an average high temperature in January of 57 degrees Fahrenheit (14 degrees Celsius). Taos, in the north, has an average high of just 40°F (4°C) in January. The northern mountains receive the most snowfall of anywhere in the state.

WORDS TO KNOW

erosion *the gradual wearing away of rock or soil by physical breakdown, chemical solution, or water*

semiarid *receiving 10 to 20 inches (25 to 50 cm) of rain every year*

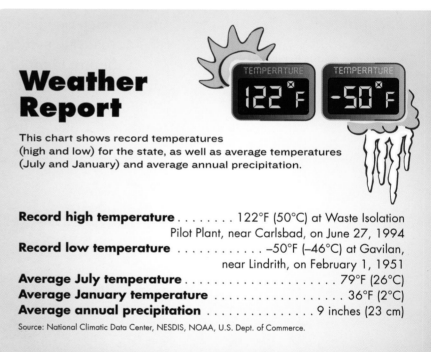

Weather Report

This chart shows record temperatures (high and low) for the state, as well as average temperatures (July and January) and average annual precipitation.

Record high temperature . . . . 122°F (50°C) at Waste Isolation Pilot Plant, near Carlsbad, on June 27, 1994
Record low temperature . . . . –50°F (–46°C) at Gavilan, near Lindrith, on February 1, 1951
Average July temperature . . . . 79°F (26°C)
Average January temperature . . . . 36°F (2°C)
Average annual precipitation . . . . 9 inches (23 cm)

Source: National Climatic Data Center, NESDIS, NOAA, U.S. Dept. of Commerce.

Some northern New Mexico mountains receive 300 inches (762 centimeters) of snow every year—enough to bury a two-story house!

Summer brings rain across the state, with the north getting the most. Powerful July and August thunderstorms dump huge amounts of rain, bringing the threat of flash floods. Normally dry riverbeds, called arroyos, fill with water and overflow their banks. These rushing waters can stop traffic and destroy roads and bridges.

PLANT LIFE

A desert might seem like a tough place for plants to live. Yet a variety of plants have adapted to the desert and semiarid regions of New Mexico. Yucca and cacti store water inside their leaves and stems for later use. Piñon, oak, and juniper trees live in the higher desert regions. The piñon, the state tree, is valued for its pine nuts, which people collect for cooking and sometimes sell at roadside stands.

Different kinds of plants are found starting at elevations of about 6,500 feet (2,000 m) in central New Mexico. Wildflowers such as columbine and pennyroyal dot the land, and Douglas firs and ponderosa pines tower over

A claret cup cactus in bloom

mountainsides. Cottonwood trees line the Rio Grande. At around 9,000 feet (2,700 m), spruce and aspen firs become more common. Pine and fir trees grow until the elevation tops about 12,000 feet (3,600 m). Above that line, only a few hardy pines and wildflowers can survive the harsh winds and cold temperatures.

New Mexico National Park Areas

This map shows some of New Mexico's national parks, monuments, preserves, and other areas protected by the National Park Service.

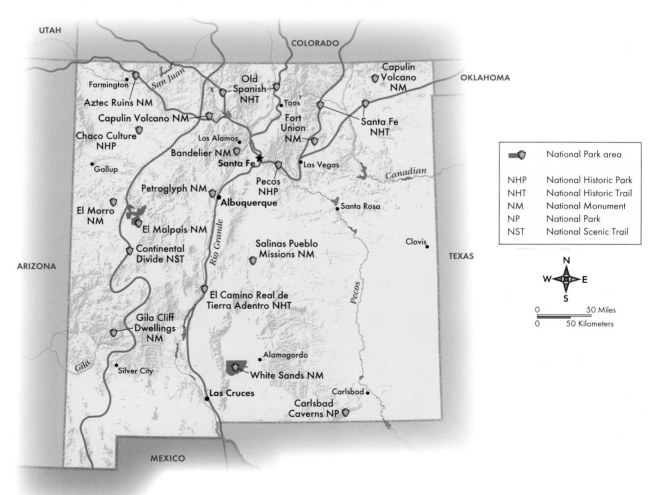

UTAH

COLORADO

OKLAHOMA

Farmington

San Juan

Old Spanish NHT

Capulin Volcano NM

Aztec Ruins NM

Capulin Volcano NM

Taos

Fort Union NM

Santa Fe NHT

Chaco Culture NHP

Los Alamos

Bandelier NM

Gallup

Santa Fe

Las Vegas

Canadian

Petroglyph NM

Pecos NHP

Albuquerque

El Morro NM

Santa Rosa

El Malpais NM

Salinas Pueblo Missions NM

Clovis

Continental Divide NST

Rio Grande

TEXAS

ARIZONA

El Camino Real de Tierra Adentro NHT

Pecos

Gila Cliff Dwellings NM

Gila

Silver City

Alamogordo

White Sands NM

Las Cruces

Carlsbad

Carlsbad Caverns NP

MEXICO

	National Park area
NHP	National Historic Park
NHT	National Historic Trail
NM	National Monument
NP	National Park
NST	National Scenic Trail

N
W E
S

0   50 Miles
0   50 Kilometers

ANIMAL LIFE

As with plants, the kinds of animals living in New Mexico vary with the climate and elevation. Desert dwellers include lizards, snakes, and poisonous tarantulas. The state bird, the roadrunner, also prefers desert regions. Pronghorn live along the edges of the desert. Otero Mesa, in southern New Mexico, has the state's largest pronghorn population. At slightly higher elevations, white-tailed deer roam. From 6,500 to 8,500 feet (2,000 to 2,500 m), common animals include black bears, elk, and wild turkeys. At the highest altitudes live bighorn sheep and ermines, relatives of the weasel.

Although New Mexico is mostly desert and rock, about one-quarter of it is forested. Gila National Forest, in the southwest, is home to more than 150 different kinds of animals. Trout, catfish, and bass swim in Gila's streams, and a variety of toads, frogs, turtles, and lizards live in and around its waters. Mammals in Gila National Forest include bats, squirrels, and mice. Less common

Pronghorn doe and fawn

The Mexican gray wolf has faced near extinction in New Mexico and other regions of the Southwest.

ENDANGERED WILDLIFE

The **endangered** Mexican spotted owl lives in New Mexico's Colorado Plateau. At almost 18 inches (46 cm) tall, it is one of the largest owls in the world. Only about 2,000 Mexican spotted owls still live in New Mexico and nearby states. Another endangered animal is the Gila monster, a lizard that lives in the desert. Gilas don't usually bother humans, but their poisonous bite can be deadly. The jaguar, the biggest cat in the Americas, is also endangered. Some jaguars move freely across the border between New Mexico and Mexico, but overall their numbers are dropping.

Mexican spotted owl

are bobcats and mountain lions. The forest also shelters more than 150 kinds of birds. These include geese, ducks, owls, and vultures. The bald eagle, the symbol of the United States, pays summer visits to the forest.

HUMANS AND THE ENVIRONMENT

Human activities, such as building houses or hunting, can harm plants and animals. Concerned New Mexicans are trying to help save endangered wildlife and their habitats. The Gila trout is one fish that has been helped by such efforts. At one time, the Gila trout population in the Southwest had fallen to about 7,500. Then the state outlawed fishing for Gila trout, and now their numbers have rebounded to about 37,000. The Mexican gray wolf was almost wiped out in the Southwest. New Mexico officials are now working with the U.S. government and neighboring states to return the wolf to its Rocky Mountain home. Other programs continue the effort to protect New Mexico's land and wildlife.

WORD TO KNOW

endangered *in danger of becoming extinct*

22

READ ABOUT

The First
Peoples of New
Mexico......24

The Anasazi
People 25

Anasazis on the
Move.......29

Newcomers
to New
Mexico......30

Ancient peoples
created these
images at
Petroglyph
National
Monument in
Albuquerque.

c. 9000 BCE

*Hunters live in the
area near Clovis*

▲ **c. 850 CE**
*The Anasazis begin
building towns in
Chaco Canyon*

c. 1000

*The Navajos and
Apaches first enter the
Southwest*

CHAPTER TWO

FIRST PEOPLE

★

TODAY, MUCH OF NEW MEXICO IS HOT AND DRY. But more than 20,000 years ago, thick sheets of ice covered much of the state, during what's called the ice age. As the ice began to melt, the first residents of New Mexico arrived. These early New Mexicans were hunters. They came to the Americas over a land bridge that once connected Alaska and Asia. Other hunters may also have come by boat.

Folsom dart point

1100

The population in Chaco Canyon reaches about 5,000

1908 ▲

George McJunkin finds bones of the Folsom people

1930s

Archaeologists find bones of the Clovis people

This dart point is made of flint and was discovered among Folsom ruins in New Mexico.

WORD TO KNOW

archaeologists *people who study the remains of past human societies*

THE FIRST PEOPLES OF NEW MEXICO

Around 11,000 years ago, a group of hunters lived in what is now Clovis, New Mexico. They used spears to hunt animals of all sizes—from giant mammoths to tiny rabbits. These hunters left behind some stone spearheads and the bones of the animals they killed for food and clothing. During the 1930s, **archaeologists** found some of those stones and bones. They named the people who left them Clovis. Other remains from the Clovis people have been found across the Southwest.

Another group of ancient hunters lived near what is now Folsom, New Mexico. The Folsom people arrived about 2,000 years after the Clovis. The Folsom also used spears to hunt, but their spearheads were slightly smaller and better made. These two groups of early New Mexicans lived in similar ways. They moved from spot to spot, following game. They also gathered wild nuts and seeds for food. They lived in caves or close to rocks that could protect them from wind and rain.

Over the centuries, the Folsom and the Clovis people left New Mexico, and new people wandered in. Meanwhile, the region became hotter and drier, causing some game animals to leave the area. The people of the Southwest needed a new source of food. Native Americans in Mexico had already learned how to farm. By around 3,500 years ago, Native New Mexicans were raising crops of corn and squash. They soon added beans to their farms.

THE ANASAZI PEOPLE

Several groups of people farmed in the Southwest. Hohokams lived in land that is now Arizona, while Mogollons lived there and in New Mexico. A later group of Mogollons lived along the Mimbres River in New Mexico. Also called Mimbres, these people created dazzling black and white pottery, often decorated with images of animals.

Another group, the Anasazi people, settled in what is called the Four Corners region—the area where New Mexico, Arizona, Colorado, and Utah now meet. The first Anasazi communities were small villages. Families lived in pit houses—homes dug in the ground and covered with logs. Anasazis learned to weave and make baskets and pottery. They wove fibers from the yucca plant with turkey feathers and strips of animal skin to

MINI-BIO

GEORGE MCJUNKIN: COWBOY SCIENTIST

George McJunkin (1851–1922) had been enslaved in Texas and had settled in New Mexico to work on a ranch. He was keenly interested in science. He even carried a telescope with him as he rode his horse! One day, he made a great discovery when he was out fixing fences. In 1908, he found bones in a fence hole. He knew the bones probably belonged to an extinct animal, and he tried to get people to visit his "bone pit." But no one would make the trip to the remote ranch. Only after McJunkin's death did experts realize the bones he found were from an ancient buffalo. The scientists went to the bone pit and also found the spearheads that led to the naming of the Folsom people.

? Want to know more? Go to www.uh.edu/engines/epi2010.htm

Native American Peoples
(Before European Contact)

This map shows the general area of Native American peoples before European settlers arrived.

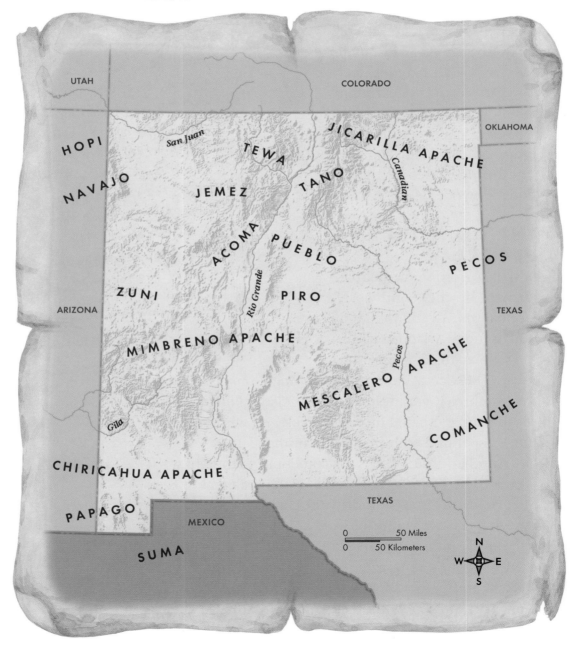

make baskets. They also improved farming methods, building dams and **reservoirs** to collect water.

Starting around 850 CE, Anasazis began to build larger towns in Chaco Canyon in what is now northwestern New Mexico. At Chaco, they built large structures out of stone and adobe, which is a mixture of sand and clay (colonists later added straw to the adobe mixture, which made it stronger). These buildings were later called pueblos, the Spanish word for "villages." Some pueblos had hundreds of rooms. Underground, Anasazis built rooms called kivas that were used for religious ceremonies. One kiva at Chaco Canyon was large enough to hold 500 people.

WORD TO KNOW

reservoirs *artificial lakes or tanks created for water storage*

The largest known pueblo was Sawape, near the Chama River. It had more 2,500 rooms on its ground floor and may have had 1,500 more on its second level.

An artist's depiction of Anasazi people working in teams to carry ponderosa pine logs from forests many miles away

SEE IT HERE!

PUEBLO BONITO

Far off the main roads of northwestern New Mexico sit the remains of Chaco Canyon. Visitors to the Chaco Culture National Historical Park can explore the ruins of Pueblo Bonito, the largest structure in the canyon. Shaped like the letter D, the four-story pueblo once had more than 600 rooms. From the canyon trails, you can look down and see the circular kivas—40 of them in all. Five other sites in the park are also open to the public.

WORD TO KNOW

rituals *religious ceremonies or social customs*

Anasazis believed all people had souls that came out of the earth, the source of all life. Kivas were built underground to represent this idea of humans emerging out of the earth. When people died, their souls returned to "Mother Earth" through the same spot where they first entered. Anasazis held **rituals** to seek help from the gods they believed watched over them.

By about 1100, the settlement in Chaco Canyon had about 5,000 people. The Anasazi people of Chaco Canyon built a series of roads to connect their pueblos with distant towns. They traded tiles made of turquoise, a blue stone, with distant tribes. In return, they received goods such as parrots, cotton, and copper bells.

The remains of Pueblo Bonito, a settlement in Chaco Canyon

ANASAZIS ON THE MOVE

By about 1300, Anasazis had left their pueblos at Chaco Canyon. A long dry spell played a part in their departure, as growing crops became harder. Disease or attacks by enemies may have caused them to leave as well.

Some Anasazis moved farther south and east. They built new pueblos, sometimes placing them in front of caves. Eventually, Anasazis built many pueblos near the Rio Grande. Families stored food and other goods on the bottom floor. Going "upstairs" to eat or sleep meant climbing up a ladder.

By about 1500, Anasazis had become several distinct groups, including the Hopi and the Zuni people. Today, these many groups together are called Pueblos, though each community has its own identity.

In Pueblo villages, men farmed and hunted, while women made pottery. Like Anasazis, the Pueblo groups held rituals in underground kivas. They shared their ancestors' belief in how humans' souls entered and left

FAQ

Q: WHAT DOES ANASAZI MEAN?

A: *Anasazi* comes from a Navajo word that is translated several different ways. It can mean "ancient ones who are not among us" or simply "ancient ones." It is also sometimes translated as "ancient enemies" or "enemy ancestors." Some modern-day Pueblos of northern New Mexico prefer to call Anasazis "**Ancestral** Puebloans," while the Hopis—another group from northern New Mexico that traces its roots to Anasazis—call them Hisatsinom—"ancient ones."

WORD TO KNOW

ancestral *relating to an ancestor, or a family member from the distant past*

Picture Yourself . . .

Making Pueblo Pottery

Pottery is important to your village, so you want to learn the craft. You watch your mother and grandmother form clay for the pots. Then the pots are hardened from the heat of a huge bonfire. You boil plants and use the residue for painting the surfaces of the pots. And you find yucca leaves to use as brushes. You try your hand at creating a beautiful pattern on your pot. And you hope one day to be as talented as those teaching you. Your pot will be used for storage or carrying water.

MINI-BIO

ALFONSO ORTIZ: SCHOLAR OF HIS PEOPLE

During his professional career, Alfonso Ortiz (1939–1997) wrote several books about the spiritual beliefs and history of the Pueblo people. Ortiz was an anthropologist—a scientist who studies the daily lives and common beliefs of people and their ancestors. He was well-suited to study Pueblos—he was a member of the San Juan Pueblo. After studying at the University of New Mexico, he earned degrees at the University of Chicago. Later in life, Ortiz returned to his home state to teach.

? Want to know more? See www.mnsu.edu/emuseum/information/biography/klmno/ortiz_alfonso.html

this world. Pueblos also believed that spirits called kachinas helped humans by bringing rain to make crops grow. Dancers wore masks that represented the different kachinas, and children received kachina dolls. The dolls helped the young learn about the role of kachinas in their life.

NEWCOMERS TO NEW MEXICO

While Anasazis farmed and built towns, other Native Americans in what is now New Mexico led much different lives. Starting around 1000, Navajos and Apaches entered the Southwest. They had originally lived in Canada and in today's northwestern United States. Navajos and Apaches spoke related languages. Both groups traveled according to the season, hunting for animals and searching for nuts and seeds. These newcomers sometimes raided Anasazi villages for food.

Navajos soon began to settle down in villages. Some adopted Anasazi ways of raising crops. They built homes called hogans out of wood and mud, and they sometimes traded with Anasazis. Over time, Navajos also learned how to farm from their new neighbors. Apaches, meanwhile, tended to stay on the move, though they also did some farming and trading. They were considered fierce fighters—their name came from a Zuni word meaning "enemy." Different bands

Pueblo women making bread in an adobe oven

of Apaches lived in west Texas, northern Mexico, and parts of New Mexico and Arizona.

The Pueblo people sometimes fought with these newcomers. Still, by the early 1500s, the Pueblo had about 80 communities across New Mexico. Soon, however, they would all face a new challenge, with the arrival of the first Europeans.

READ ABOUT

Searching for
Cibola 34

The Pueblo
Revolt 38

Reconquest . . . 40

A Frontier
Land 40

Estevanico exploring the region that became the American Southwest

1539 ►
Marcos de Niza and Estevanico lead the first Spanish expedition into New Mexico

1598
Juan de Oñate leads Spanish settlers to the Rio Grande valley

1610
Santa Fe becomes the capital of New Mexico

CHAPTER THREE

EXPLORATION AND SETTLEMENT

★

I N 1528, A FORMER ENSLAVED AFRICAN NAMED ESTEVANICO EMBARKED ON A JOURNEY. He joined a group of 400 men who left Cuba, an island in the Caribbean Sea, in search of gold in what is now Florida. After facing storms and starvation and fighting with Native peoples, the group dwindled. Finally, only Estevanico and three others remained. They wandered the Southwest for years.

1680 ►
Pueblos rebel and drive the Spanish from New Mexico

1692
Spain regains control of New Mexico

1821
New Mexico becomes part of the independent nation of Mexico

This map shows the locations of Mexico and New Spain.

SEARCHING FOR CÍBOLA

Estevanico showed great skill learning Native American languages and living off the land. Talking with various peoples, he heard many tales of Cíbola, the fabled "seven cities of gold," which Native Americans said lay north of Mexico.

In 1538, the four men finally reached Mexico City, the capital of New Spain, the Spanish colony in North America. Estevanico's tales of Cíbola excited Don Antonio de Mendoza, the viceroy of New Spain. The following year, Mendoza named Father Marcos de Niza, an Italian priest, to head an expedition to the north. Estevanico became the mission's advance scout.

The African and his Native guides headed north toward Cíbola. From time to time, Estevanico sent Native American messengers back to de Niza, indicating his progress. Then his messages stopped. The priest waited for days for word from his scout. Finally, two Indians staggered into de Niza's camp to report that Estevanico had been killed near the Zuni village of Hawikuh. Father de Niza continued to travel northward until he claimed he saw a village made of gold. Fearing that he would suffer Estevanico's fate, he turned around and headed back to Mexico City. There he reported that he had found the seven cities of gold.

De Niza's tales stirred New Spain's rulers to further explorations. In 1540, Francisco Vásquez de Coronado, a governor in northern Mexico, planned a search for Cíbola. He gathered a group of nearly 300 Spanish soldiers, 800 Native Americans, and an unknown number of Africans. Coronado never found Cíbola, only sunny villages and stone and adobe buildings. Coronado reported that Father de Niza "has not told the truth in a single thing he said." Coronado's march established no settlements, but he claimed the Southwest for Spain. By the 1560s, settlers in New Spain were calling the land to their north New Mexico. Several decades would pass before the Spanish began settling the region.

FOUNDING SANTA FE

In 1595, Juan de Oñate, a wealthy merchant and mine owner in New Spain, set out to establish his country's first colony in the Southwest. He stated that his goal was to convert the Native people to Christianity. In 1598, Oñate led 130 soldiers, their wives, children and

FAQ

Q8 WHAT WERE THE SEVEN CITIES OF CÍBOLA?

A8 During the 16th century, many Spaniards believed that seven Roman Catholic priests had left Europe centuries earlier and founded seven cities filled with gold. The Spanish explorers of New Mexico thought that the land called Cíbola contained these seven cities.

DEMANDING JUSTICE

In 1600, when Juan Guerra de Resa led reinforcements to Juan de Oñate in New Mexico, his expedition included more Africans. One was Isabel de Olvera, a free, unmarried woman of Native American and African ancestry. Concerned about her safety on a frontier dominated by European officers and soldiers, she appeared before Don Pedro Lorenzo de Castilla, a local mayor, to request a document of legal protection. Her defiant statement is the first protest by a person of African descent in the Americas. It ended with "I demand justice."

SEE IT HERE!

EL MORRO

While in New Mexico, Juan de Oñate led several expeditions across the Southwest. On their way back from one trip, Oñate and his men spied a mesa now called El Morro—meaning, in English, "the bluff." Travelers often stopped at El Morro to drink from a pool of freshwater that collected there. About 700 years ago, the Anasazis had built two pueblos on top of the towering rock. They also carved pictures, called petroglyphs, into its base. Like the Anasazis, the Spaniards left carvings in the rock. They wrote in Spanish, "Passed by here the Governor Don Juan de Oñate . . . on the 16th of April, 1605." Later, other Spaniards and Americans also left messages in the rock. Today, El Morro is a national monument, and you can still see the ancient petroglyphs and carvings.

servants, and 10 priests north. They were followed by 83 wagons, along with carts, pack mules, pigs, goats, sheep, and 7,000 cattle that would serve as food. The caravan stretched for almost 4 miles (6 km). When he crossed the Rio Grande into what is now Texas, Oñate proclaimed a day of celebration. There were patriotic speeches and religious services. Trumpets blared and banners waved.

After the party came harsh reality. Spain's soldiers charged into a nearby pueblo. They forced the people out and took over their homes. For two months, Oñate's forces pushed northward. Finally, they set up a headquarters near the Rio Grande, some 20 miles (32 km) from today's Santa Fe. Oñate's soldiers forced the Pueblo people to convert to Christianity. They demanded that the Native people provide them with food, clothing, and labor. Many Native people fled into the countryside.

Weary of the brutality, the Acomas attacked the Spanish settlers. In response, Oñate ordered a three-day assault on Acoma villages. About 800 Acomas were killed, including women and children. Oñate ordered his soldiers to round up 80 Native men and 500 Native women and children. Those aged 12 to 25 were sentenced to 20 years of forced labor. Children under 12 were taken from their parents and placed in the care of priests.

Exploration of New Mexico

The colored arrows on this map show the routes taken by pioneers and explorers between 1539 and 1846.

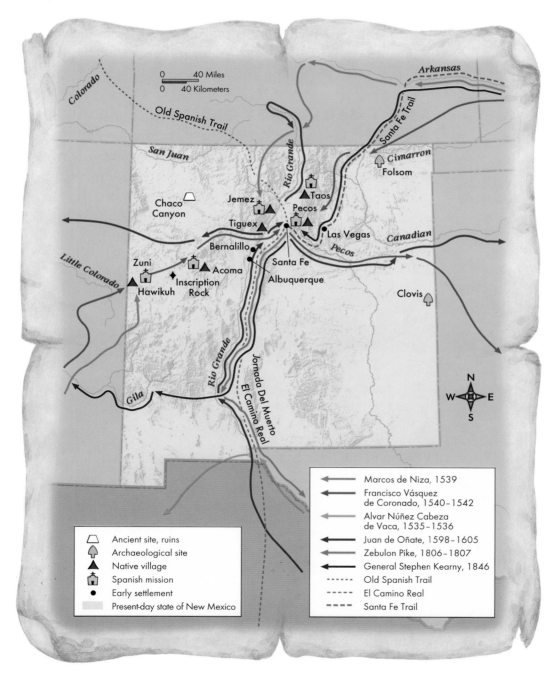

Colorado

0 — 40 Miles
0 — 40 Kilometers

Arkansas

Old Spanish Trail

Santa Fe Trail

San Juan

Rio Grande

Cimarron
Folsom

Chaco
Canyon

Jemez

Taos

Pecos

Tiguex

Las Vegas

Canadian

Bernalillo

Pecos

Zuni

Acoma

Santa Fe

Little Colorado

Hawikuh

Inscription
Rock

Albuquerque

Clovis

Gila

Rio Grande

Jornada Del Muerto
El Camino Real

N
W · E
S

Ancient site, ruins
Archaeological site
Native village
Spanish mission
Early settlement
Present-day state of New Mexico

Marcos de Niza, 1539
Francisco Vásquez
de Coronado, 1540–1542
Alvar Núñez Cabeza
de Vaca, 1535–1536
Juan de Oñate, 1598–1605
Zebulon Pike, 1806–1807
General Stephen Kearny, 1846
Old Spanish Trail
El Camino Real
Santa Fe Trail

In 1610, construction of the Palace of the Governors in Santa Fe began. Today, it is the oldest surviving government building in the United States.

The Palace of the Governors in Santa Fe, which became the capitol of New Mexico

Finally, Oñate ordered that 80 Acoma men aged 25 and older each have their left foot cut off.

Oñate continued in his brutal campaign. Finally, in 1610, Pedro de Peralta arrived to succeed Oñate as governor of New Mexico. By then, most of the settlers had moved farther south. The settlers called their new town Santa Fe, and Peralta moved New Mexico's capital there.

THE PUEBLO REVOLT

The Spaniards had promised the Pueblo villagers that if they became Christian, they would have healthy crops and enough food. When this did not happen, village elders called for a return to traditional religion. In 1675, Spanish officials hanged three Pueblo religious leaders

A scene from the Pueblo revolt against the Spaniards in 1680

Picture Yourself . . .

as a Pueblo When the Spanish Arrive

With the arrival of the Spanish, your old life disappeared. Spanish **missionaries** and soldiers speak to you in Spanish and do not bother to learn your language. They force your father and mother to work away from home and without pay, raising crops for the Spaniards, while your village's crops die. You are not allowed to ride horses. You cannot practice your religion or take part in kachina dances. Instead, you have to follow the religion of the Spaniards. The suffering you see around you explains why some Pueblo leaders decide to rebel against the Spaniards in 1680.

who called for a return to ancient spiritual ways. They whipped 43 others.

One of the people who was whipped was named Popé. He was a master of military tactics and dedicated to the Pueblo people. He and other Pueblo leaders decided to drive out the foreign rulers and return to the ancient ways. They spent five years designing their plan. They recruited 17,000 people in dozens of villages spread over hundreds of miles. The Pueblo peoples spoke many different languages, but Popé managed to unite them.

WORD TO KNOW

missionaries *people who try to convert others to a religion*

The revolt was set for August 1680. It began with Pueblo people swooping down on Spanish settlements along the Rio Grande. Settlers fled their farms and homes and poured into Santa Fe. Popé soon captured Santa Fe and then allowed the Spaniards to flee to El Paso, Texas. After the Pueblos drove out the foreigners, Popé said no one could speak Spanish, use Spanish tools, or practice Christianity. The Pueblo Revolt of 1680 destroyed the Spanish hold in the region—for the time being.

RECONQUEST

More than a decade passed before Spaniards tried to regain their New Mexican colony. In 1692, Diego de Vargas marched north from El Paso with about 200 troops. He knew he could not defeat the Pueblo, so he used prayer and kind words to try to win their favor. De Vargas said the Spaniards would not harm the Indians if they agreed to accept Spanish rule again. Most agreed, and Vargas was considered the hero of the *reconquista*, or the reconquest, of New Mexico. Settlers returned to their old homes. Some Pueblo people resisted, but by the end of the century the Spaniards were firmly in control. Many Pueblos were allowed to follow a mix of their old beliefs and Catholic teachings.

A FRONTIER LAND

In the early 1700s, some New Mexicans began moving away from these original towns and founding new settlements. Albuquerque was first settled in 1706, as 30 families moved south from the town of Bernalillo. They built adobe houses and a church in their new home.

SEE IT HERE!

OLD TOWN ALBUQUERQUE

The first Spanish settlers of Albuquerque lived in what is now called Old Town. This western section of the city near the Rio Grande still has some original adobe buildings. Many of them now house shops and restaurants. New Mexicans flock to Old Town for its Christmas celebration, when hundreds of thousands of *farolitos* (candles placed inside bags weighed down with sand) light up the neighborhood. Old Town is also said to have a ghost or two, and visitors can tour supposedly haunted sites.

By the 1730s, French traders had entered Santa Fe. Spanish officials had always seen New Mexico as a "wall" to keep the French and other Europeans out of New Spain. The Mexican mines produced large amounts of silver. So Spain's rulers had feared that the French or other Europeans would someday seek the wealth of New Spain. Spanish officials told the French traders to stay out of New Mexico. The New Mexicans, however, welcomed the traders. They brought cloth and other goods that were hard to get from Mexico City.

WORLD EVENTS

In 1783, after fighting the Revolutionary War, American colonies on the East Coast earned their independence from Great Britain. Then, in 1803, President Thomas Jefferson bought the Louisiana Territory from France. That vast territory bordered the region that was controlled by Spain, and it included the northeast section of present-day New Mexico. By 1810, colonists in New Spain were demanding independence from Spain. After a long struggle, in 1821 the new nation of Mexico was born. New Mexico was now part of that new nation.

Louisiana Purchase

This map shows the area (in yellow) that made up the Louisiana Purchase and the present-day state of New Mexico (in orange).

British Possessions

Louisiana Purchase

Spanish Possessions

N W E S

United States, 1803

Louisiana Purchase

United States Territory, 1803

Present-day state of New Mexico

READ ABOUT

The Anglos
Arrive 44

The Mexican
War 45

Life as
Americans. . . . 46

The Civil
War 47

Time of
Growth 50

Pueblo villagers
and their adobe
homes

1821

William Becknell opens
the Santa Fe Trail

1846 ▲

U.S. forces invade
New Mexico

1850

New Mexico
becomes a U.S.
territory

CHAPTER FOUR

GROWTH AND CHANGE

★

I N THE EARLY 19TH CENTURY, LIFE IN NEW MEXICO DID NOT CHANGE VERY MUCH. Most people still lived in simple adobe homes. And many people went to the yearly trade fair in Taos to buy goods they couldn't make or get from Mexico. For centuries, Native people had been gathering there to trade, and the Spanish shared that tradition.

1862
Union and
Confederate forces
battle at Glorieta Pass

1878
Fighting between
ranchers and merchants
erupts in Lincoln County

1912 ▶
New Mexico
becomes the
47th state

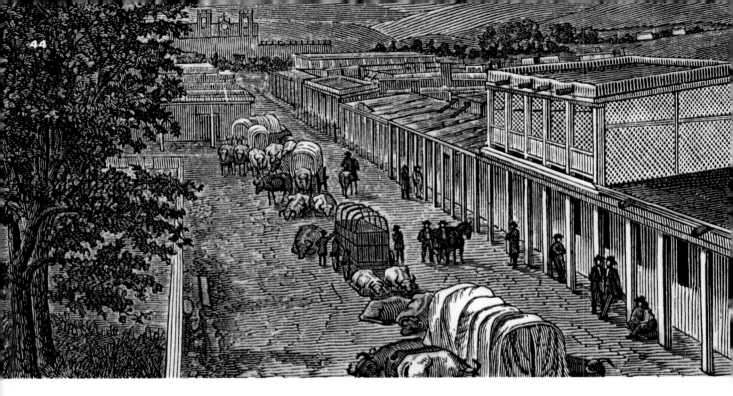

This woodcut shows a group of settlers in covered wagons arriving in Santa Fe.

Q: WHAT IS AN ANGLO?

A: In 19th-century New Mexico, an Anglo was an American who settled in the region. The word can be traced back to Anglia, the Latin name for England. Over time, the term *Anglo* also referred to any white immigrant who came to New Mexico. Today, *Anglo* can mean a white person, whether born in New Mexico or not. It is used to distinguish European heritage from the Mexican and Native American traditions in the state.

THE ANGLOS ARRIVE

With the end of Spanish rule, great changes came to New Mexico. Traders from the United States and European nations could now freely enter New Mexico. One of the first American traders to arrive was William Becknell. He and about 20 other men left Missouri in September 1821 with goods to trade in New Mexico. They were greeted warmly. Becknell quickly sold all his goods and then returned the next year with much more. The route Becknell followed west across the Great Plains to New Mexico was soon called the Santa Fe Trail. Until the 1870s, it was the main route between New Mexico and the eastern United States.

At first, relations between the Anglos and local people were peaceful. But soon, slaveholding Americans arrived in the region. Slavery was illegal in Mexico. Anglos in New Mexico were in constant disagreement with the Mexican government over the use of slave labor. Real trouble erupted in 1836 after

Anglos in Texas succeeded in a revolution for independence from Mexico. Mexican officials feared that Anglos in New Mexico might get similar ideas.

Suspicions rose higher when Texas became part of the United States in 1845. By then, U.S. president James Polk already planned to expand U.S. territory in the Southwest. He wanted to take over California, another part of Mexico. In May 1846, the United States declared war on its southern neighbor. U.S. troops soon invaded New Mexico.

THE MEXICAN WAR

Some wealthy New Mexicans decided to work with the Americans. They surrendered at the start of the war. But Pueblos

The U.S. Army capturing Santa Fe in 1846

and mixed-race Mexicans resisted U.S. control. In January 1847, a group of rebels killed Charles Bent, Stephen Kearney's appointed governor, and fled for safety to the Taos Pueblo church. The U.S. Army opened fire with cannons, destroying the church and killing many of the rebels.

The Taos rebellion was the last major violence in New Mexico during the Mexican War. The war ended in May 1848 with a U.S. victory. The United States took over New Mexico, California, and other Mexican lands in the Southwest. In 1850, New Mexico became a U.S. territory, a first step toward its becoming a state.

The territory included today's Arizona and parts of Colorado and Nevada. Three years later, the United States bought a small strip of land from Mexico that also became part of New Mexico. This land, called the Gadsden Purchase, set the current border between Mexico and the United States.

LIFE AS AMERICANS

Being part of the United States wasn't always easy for New Mexicans. Few of them spoke English. In addition, most New Mexicans were Roman Catholic at a time when the majority of Americans were Protestant. Many Americans were also **prejudiced** against Native

WORD TO KNOW

prejudiced *having an unreasonable hatred or fear of others*

Most New Mexicans, like those seen here at the San Miguel Mission in Santa Fe, practiced Roman Catholicism.

Americans and mixed-race Mexicans. They didn't think they had the political skills or intelligence to govern themselves. For more than 62 years, these racist ideas kept New Mexico from becoming a state.

Most of the first Americans who went to New Mexico were soldiers. They built forts to defend residents from Native American attacks. The first U.S. fort built in New Mexico was Fort Union. It sat where two branches of the Santa Fe Trail met before heading to the capital.

One early arrival to New Mexico was Jean Baptiste Lamy, a bishop in the Roman Catholic Church. Lamy had been born in France, but had lived in the United States for about 10 years. He helped build dozens of new churches, as well as hospitals and schools. These schools gave many young New Mexicans their first lessons in English and Anglo culture. Novelist Willa Cather based the title character in her classic novel *Death Comes for the Archbishop* on Lamy.

THE CIVIL WAR

In the 1850s, the issue of slavery divided the United States. Slave owners and others believed that the people living in new states and territories should be allowed to decide for themselves whether to allow slavery. Others, mostly Northerners, wanted to limit slavery to where it already existed. A smaller third group said slavery should be **abolished** everywhere in the United States.

In 1860, New Mexico's total population was 93,516. Only 85 were African Americans. The vast majority of white settlers did not own slaves and were opposed to slaveholding, but they were not supportive of African Americans living in their region. By 1860, white New Mexicans had passed a series of laws that denied African Americans the right to vote or serve on juries.

WORD TO KNOW

abolished *put an end to*

The remains of Fort Union, the first
U.S. fort built in New Mexico

SOLDIER IN DISGUISE

Cathay Williams (1842–1924) was born into slavery in
Missouri. After the Civil War began, U.S. troops forced her
to serve as their cook. She traveled all over the South with
the army and in 1866 decided to join the military herself.
Since women could not enter the military at that time, she
dressed as a man and called herself William. No officer
realized that he was actually a she! The U.S. Army sent
Williams to New Mexico, where she served with the Buffalo
Soldiers, African American troops who fought Native
Americans in the Great Plains and Southwest.

The slavery issue led 11 Southern states to leave
the United States and form a new nation called the
Confederate States of America. In
1861, the Civil War began as North
and South fought over whether
the Southern states could leave
the Union. New Mexicans were
split about whose side to support.
People in the northern part of the
state largely supported the Union.
Many people who lived in southern New Mexico had once lived
in Texas, a Confederate state, and
they supported the Confederacy.

The war soon reached New Mexico. By February 1862, Confederate troops were advancing toward Fort Craig, near Socorro. There they met a Union force that included many Hispanic volunteers from New Mexico and the famed frontiersman Kit Carson. The Confederates won the Battle of Valverde and moved on to take Albuquerque and Santa Fe. Their next goal was Fort Union. Before the Confederates reached the fort, Union forces marched down the Santa Fe Trail and met them at Glorieta Pass. Although the Confederates at first won the battle, Union soldiers managed to destroy the Confederates' supply train. The Confederate troops soon realized they could not win in New Mexico and left the territory.

As the Civil War raged in the East, a new tolerance blossomed in New Mexico. Fugitive slaves were not stopped or arrested at its border. Many found freedom, friends, and a home on the frontier, and some even made a fortune.

Once the Confederate troops had left New Mexico, U.S. officials made plans to bring the Navajo and Apache people under military control. Kit Carson led the effort to round up Mescalero Apaches and force them onto a reservation. Carson also destroyed Navajo crops and livestock. By 1868, the Navajos had given up all their guns and ended their raids on U.S. settlements.

MINI-BIO

KIT CARSON: TRAPPER, SCOUT, SOLDIER

Christopher "Kit" Carson (1809–1868) became the most famous American to settle in New Mexico during Mexican rule. A native of Kentucky, Carson joined a wagon train heading west in 1826. He spent time in Taos before becoming a trapper and hunter in the Rocky Mountains. His outdoor skills became legendary, and he worked as a scout for U.S. explorers and soldiers in the West. In 1862, he commanded New Mexicans fighting for the North during the Civil War. Today, some people remember him for his brutal treatment of the Apaches and Navajos during the 1860s.

? Want to know more? Go to: www.pbs.org/weta/thewest/people/a_c/carson.htm

At the Battle of Glorieta Pass, volunteers from Colorado marched more than 170 miles (274 km) through deep snow in just five days to help New Mexican soldiers fight the Confederate troops.

BILLY THE KID: NOT KIDDING AROUND

Gunslinger William Bonney (1859?–1881), better known as Billy the Kid, helped New Mexico earn its "Wild West" reputation. Billy was born in New York City. He arrived in Silver City, New Mexico, in 1873, after years of moving around the country. In 1878, he took part in the Lincoln County War, which pitted ranchers against merchants. He killed several men and was sent to jail, but he later escaped. He died in a gunfight at Fort Sumner, New Mexico, in 1881.

? **Want to know more?** See www.crimelibrary.com/ americana/kid/

WOW

New Mexico has more than 400 ghost towns. Several former ghost towns have been turned into tourist attractions.

TIME OF GROWTH

In the decades after the Civil War, more settlers headed to New Mexico. Most came hoping to make money. Miners arrived with picks and shovels to dig up silver, copper, lead, coal, and other minerals. New towns such as Elizabethtown and Silver City sprang up near the mines. Socorro had a population of 4,500 in 1889, making it one of the largest towns in the territory. Some of the new "boom towns" died quickly. When the minerals ran out in the nearby hills, the miners moved on, leaving behind "ghost towns" filled with empty buildings.

Ranching also became big business in New Mexico. Ranchers from Texas brought cattle to graze on grassland in eastern New Mexico. John Chisum of Roswell hired 100 cowboys to take care of his large herd. On cattle drives, the cowboys led thousands of head of cattle to market. Many of the cowboys were Mexican Americans, Native Americans, and African Americans.

Miners and ranchers needed an easy way to transport their goods, and railroads provided the answer. By 1881, two major rail lines cut through the territory, including the Atchison, Topeka, and Santa Fe. As tracks were laid, towns competed to get a station. Having a railroad stop brought in new businesses and jobs.

Men seeking quick riches in these new towns sometimes ignored the law, and some outlaws were ready to settle arguments with guns. New Mexico sat at the heart of the Wild West. Cimarron was a particularly rowdy town, where killings were common.

Battles with Native Americans added to the violence. In New Mexico and throughout the Southwest, African American troops called Buffalo Soldiers were the only people keeping order. They fought cattle thieves, protected farmers, and tried to keep the peace between Native Americans and white settlers.

In New Mexico, U.S. troops fought the Kiowas and the Comanches, Native groups who lived on the southern Great Plains. They also tracked down bands of Chiricahua Apaches who had refused to join other Apaches on New Mexico reservations. One of the rebels was a valiant Apache leader named Geronimo, who for decades tried to defend his people against the loss of Native lands to the U.S. government. By 1890, the Indian Wars of the Southwest were

FAQ

Q8 WHAT WAS THE "LONG WALK" OF THE NAVAJOS?

A8 After Kit Carson's invasion of their lands, the Navajos were forced to go to eastern New Mexico. In the winter of 1864, the Navajos walked 300 miles (500 km) to reach a reservation in southeastern New Mexico. Along the way, U.S. troops killed Navajos who were too weak to continue. After several years on the reservation, where they suffered from starvation and disease, the Navajos convinced U.S. officials to let them return to their traditional home in the Four Corners region. Today, Navajos consider their "Long Walk" the worst moment in their history.

Geronimo, on the horse at left, with other members of the Chiricahua Apaches

52

MINI-BIO

SUSAN WALLACE: OLD WEST WRITER

In 1879, Susan Wallace (1830–1907) went to New Mexico from Indiana to join her husband, General Lew Wallace. He had recently been named the governor of the territory. Susan was not impressed with Santa Fe, which she called "worn out." But she developed an interest in the lives of the Pueblo people. In 1888, she published a book called *The Land of the Pueblos*. She described how the Pueblo women pounded their clothes with rocks to clean them. She also wrote about finding a hidden room in the Palace of the Governors filled with records from colonial Spain. *The Land of the Pueblos* is valued today for its glimpse at New Mexico history.

? Want to know more? See crm.cr.nps.gov/archive/20-11/20-11-3.pdf

WORD TO KNOW

cavalry *soldiers who ride on horseback*

over, and the Wild West became more settled than wild.

As railroads created jobs, more people migrated to New Mexico. Immigrants arrived from all over Europe, including central European Jews, Irish Catholics, and other Anglos. African Americans arrived to work on the railroads. Asians came from the West Coast. Hispanics, many related to New Mexico's first Spanish settlers, remained the largest part of the population through the 19th century.

THE ROAD TO STATEHOOD

In 1898, the United States declared war on Spain. U.S. leaders supported rebels in Cuba who wanted independence from Spanish rule. Some Hispanic New Mexicans saw the war as their chance to prove they could be good Americans. Teddy Roosevelt, a future U.S. president, wanted to lead a **cavalry** unit to fight in Cuba. When he called for volunteers, hundreds of New Mexicans—many Hispanic—eagerly signed up. They became members of the Rough Riders. With their bravery, they proved New Mexicans' loyalty to the Union.

Over the next decade, Anglo control was fully established over New Mexico's largely Mexican and Native American population. Demands to make New Mexico a state grew. Finally, on January 6, 1912, New Mexico became the 47th state in the Union.

New Mexico: From Territory to Statehood

(1850–1912)

This map shows the original New Mexico territory and the area that became the state of New Mexico in 1912.

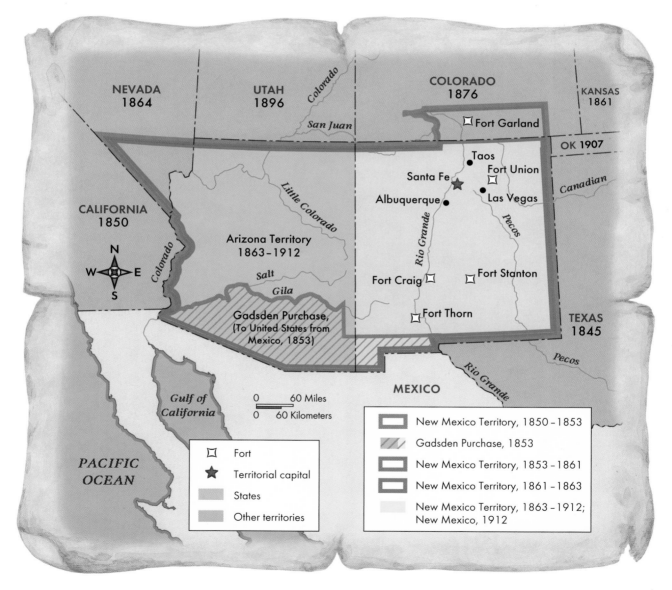

READ ABOUT

Hard
Times 57

Boom
Times 58

Postwar
Growth 61

New Mexico
Today 62

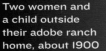

Two women and a child outside their adobe ranch home, about 1900

1916

Mexican rebel Pancho Villa raids Columbus, New Mexico

1930s

New Deal programs provide jobs for New Mexicans

▲1941–1945

During World War II, 400,000 Mexican Americans serve in the U.S. military

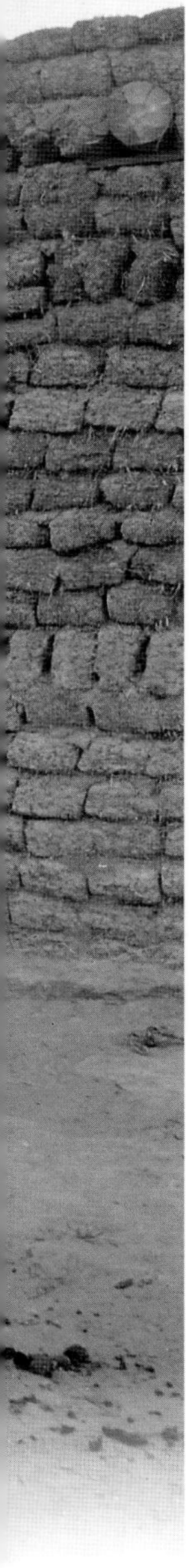

CHAPTER FIVE

MORE MODERN TIMES

★

ABOUT 300,000 PEOPLE CALLED NEW MEXICO HOME WHEN IT BECAME A STATE. For some, life had not changed much for centuries. The Pueblo people still farmed and herded, as did many Hispanic families in remote villages. But the 20th century would soon bring many changes, including a huge population boom.

1945
The world's first atomic bomb is tested at the Trinity site

1948 ▲
Miguel Trujillo helps New Mexican Indians win the right to vote

2006
Plans begin for building a fence between New Mexico and Mexico

Pancho Villa (left) at the head of his rebel army in 1916

WAR COMES TO NEW MEXICO

By the early 20th century, revolution came once more to Mexico. The U.S. government backed the Mexican government. Warfare spread over the U.S. border in 1916, when a Mexican rebel leader named Pancho Villa raided a U.S. Army base in Columbus, New Mexico.

As conditions in Mexico worsened, men and women fled to the United States seeking jobs. Employers in the United States eagerly hired the newcomers at low wages. The number of immigrants increased in each decade. In New Mexico, many became railroad workers, farmers, or miners. Some formed labor unions and went on strike for higher pay and better working conditions.

Some Mexican Americans had already begun to climb political ladders. In 1915, the people of New Mexico elected Benigno Hernández to the U.S. House of Representatives. In 1917, Ezequiel Cabeza de Baca was elected governor of New Mexico. Octaviano Larrazolo, who was born in Mexico, became governor in 1918. He was elected to the U.S. Senate a decade later. Dennis Chavez entered the Senate in 1935 and served for 27 years, rising to chairman of the powerful Public Works Committee.

HARD TIMES

In the 1920s, much of the United States thrived. Factories pumped out goods, and workers bought new products such as cars, radios, and refrigerators. New Mexico, however, was one of the poorest states in the nation. Things got even worse after 1929, when the country was plunged into the Great Depression. Factories closed, which forced millions of people out of work. When banks went out of business, people lost their life savings. As jobs disappeared, U.S. government officials moved to deport thousands of Mexican immigrants, legal and illegal, from New Mexico, Texas, Arizona, and California, as well as other Americans of Mexican descent.

MINI-BIO

ADELINA OTERO-WARREN: AN EARLY LEADER

When New Mexico became a state, women could not vote. Adelina "Nina" Otero-Warren (1881–1965) led the fight for woman suffrage. Her family's roots in New Mexico stretched back to colonial Spain. In 1914, Otero-Warren became a leader in the woman suffrage movement. Her pleas appealed to both Anglos and Hispanics. In 1917, she became one of the first female government officials in New Mexico, serving as the chairperson of the state board of health. Otero-Warren remained active as a businesswoman, writer, and political activist for the rest of her long life.

? **Want to know more?** See http://museumofthe americanwest.org/explore/exhibits/suffrage/oterowarren_full.html

WORD TO KNOW

suffrage *the right to vote*

MINI-BIO

ROBERT GODDARD: THE ROCKET MAN

Robert Goddard (1882–1945) was a brilliant man. While many New Mexicans struggled during the Great Depression, he worked to develop rockets. As a teen, Goddard had daydreamed about a craft that could carry him to Mars. As an adult, his research convinced him that rockets were the answer. In his home state of Massachusetts, he tested a small rocket in 1926. It was the first rocket ever powered by liquid fuel. In 1930, Goddard moved to Roswell, New Mexico, where he built and tested bigger and better liquid-fueled rockets. His inventions there included devices that kept rockets flying straight after they were launched. Today, Goddard is hailed as one of the greatest U.S. inventors ever.

? Want to know more? See www-istp.gsfc.nasa.gov/stargaze/Sgoddard.htm

In 1932, Franklin D. Roosevelt was elected president. Roosevelt had a plan, known as the New Deal, to help Americans during the Great Depression. One New Deal program, the Civilian Conservation Corps (CCC), gave people jobs building roads and dams, planting trees, and taking care of national lands. Almost one-third of New Mexico's land belonged to the U.S. government, so it needed many CCC workers. They built the first road at Bandelier National Monument and also built some of New Mexico's state parks. Keeping the workers supplied with food and services created jobs for other New Mexicans.

Other programs helped Hispanic farmers in northern New Mexico stay on their own lands. This preserved a way of life in the mountains that dated back to Spanish rule.

BOOM TIMES

In 1939, World War II began in Europe. Two years later, the United States entered the war. The war effort brought an end to the Great Depression. Millions of workers got jobs in factories that manufactured weapons and other goods for the U.S. government. In New

Corporal Henry Bahe Jr. (left) and Private First Class George H. Kirk were code talkers during World War II.

Mexico, there was work mining coal, copper, and uranium. World War II made immigrants from Mexico welcome again in the southwestern states. Some Mexicans came to work in the mines and on the railroads. Others arrived to do farmwork for little money.

During World War II, 400,000 Mexican Americans served in the armed forces. No other American ethnic group had a higher percentage of people serving in the war—and receiving medals. Many men from New Mexico saw combat as a way to prove their patriotism. Many volunteered as frontline troops.

Some Navajo men served as "code talkers" during World War II. Almost no non-Navajos spoke the Navajo language, so these men made a code using their own language. They used this code to send important military messages over the radio. The Navajos' code was never broken.

During the war, scientists worked on the secret Manhattan Project at Los Alamos, a site just outside Santa Fe. The goal of the Manhattan Project was to develop the first atomic bomb, which would then be used to help end the war. In 1945, atomic bombs were dropped on two Japanese cities, Hiroshima and Nagasaki, killing more than 220,000 people. Japan surrendered soon after, ending World War II.

The scientific work in Los Alamos led to other military projects in the state, and some of America's greatest scientists went to New Mexico. Several air bases were built, and the Sandia National Laboratory near Albuquerque became an important military lab. Farther south, missiles and rockets were tested at the White Sands Missile Range.

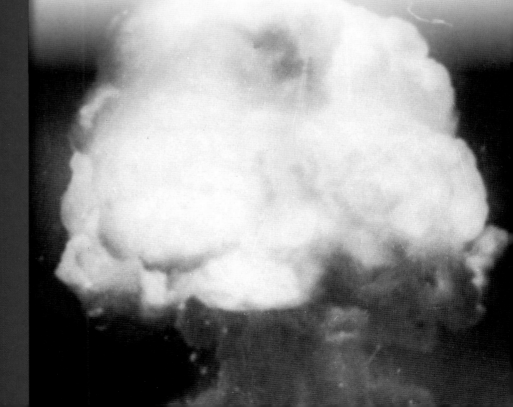

The mushroom cloud from the first atomic bomb, during a test in Alamogordo, 1945

THE BIG TEST

Manhattan Project leader J. Robert Oppenheimer chose a site near Alamogordo, east of Socorro, to test the first atomic bomb. He called the site Trinity. On July 16, 1945, the world's first atomic bomb exploded there. A huge ball of fire shot up 40,000 feet (12,000 m) over the New Mexico desert. A few weeks later, two atomic bombs were dropped on Japan. The "atomic age" had begun. People still debate whether the bombs should have been dropped.

Motels such as this one in Tucumcari accommodated the many tourists who went to New Mexico in the 1950s.

POSTWAR GROWTH

After World War II ended, scientists and others continued to go to New Mexico to work on military projects. The state's population grew rapidly.

Arts and tourism also attracted people to New Mexico. Artists first started going to Taos in the 1890s. They loved the landscape and the colors of the desert. More painters and writers arrived after World War I, and even more came after World War II.

Tourists had been visiting New Mexico for decades. The arrival of the railroad during the 1880s brought the first visitors. Many of them were interested in learning about the state's Native Americans, as well as their traditional crafts. Later, automobiles brought more travelers. In the 1950s, many new roads were built, giving travelers even more freedom to roam the state.

FAQ

Q8 WHY DID ALBUQUERQUE BECOME NEW MEXICO'S LARGEST CITY?

A8 The Sandia and Los Alamos laboratories and other businesses connected to the military attracted workers to Albuquerque from all over the United States. In 1940, the city's population was just over 35,000. Only 15 years later, it had jumped to 175,000!

MIGUEL TRUJILLO: A DETERMINED VOTER

For decades, Native Americans in New Mexico struggled to attain political rights. The New Mexico government prevented Native Americans on reservations from voting in state and federal elections. That upset Miguel Trujillo (1904–1989). He had served in the U.S. Marines and was a teacher at the Laguna Pueblo. In 1948, he tried to register to vote at the Valencia County Courthouse, but was not allowed. He then took the state to court, claiming that he and other New Mexican Indians had the right to vote since they were U.S. citizens. A state court agreed, making Trujillo a champion of democracy.

? Want to know more? See www.governor.state.ut.us/lt_gover/histofvotingrights.html

A worker on an oil rig in southeastern New Mexico

WORD TO KNOW

undocumented *lacking documents required for legal immigration or residence*

NEW MEXICO TODAY

The defense industry continues to provide jobs for many New Mexicans. Many private companies have also moved to the state, including high-tech firms that build silicon chips, the "brains" of personal computers.

New Mexico has attracted many newcomers in recent decades, including **undocumented** Mexicans who cross the border into the United States. People across the United States have debated the effects of illegal immigration. Since New Mexico shares a border with Mexico, the issue is close to home. Starting in 2006, hundreds of National Guard troops were sent to Deming to patrol the border. The federal government also made plans to build a fence along part of the border. Governor Bill Richardson said, "The fence is very unpopular on the border in Texas and New Mexico." He said it "gets in the way" of good relations between the United States and Mexico.

Illegal immigration will remain a major issue for New Mexico. So will education. In 2006, the state ranked 48th out of the 50 states in how much it spent on education. But the state is rich in oil, natural gas, and other resources. Income earned from those resources will provide New Mexico with funds for education and other important programs. As 2007 began, Richardson told New Mexicans, "The state of New Mexico is on the move, and in the right direction. We know that our best days are yet to come."

Roswell Army Air Field

MINI-BIO   63

ANNIE DODGE WAUNEKA: LIFE SAVER

The Navajos, like all Native Americans, have often faced hard times on their reservations. Improving health care was a great need. Annie Dodge Wauneka (1910–1997) played a large part in making sure the Navajos had modern medical care. Born in Arizona, she attended school in Albuquerque. Her father was a Navajo tribal leader, and she often traveled with him in New Mexico to visit Navajo villages. In 1951, she followed her father onto the Navajo Tribal Council, and she made health issues her top concern. She considered tuberculosis—an infection that attacks the lungs—the number-one enemy. By making sure Navajos received medical care, she is thought to have saved the lives of 2,000 people. Her efforts won her the Presidential Medal of Freedom in 1963.

? Want to know more? See www.greatwomen.org/women.php?action=viewone&id=166

READ ABOUT

Cities, Villages,
Nations 66

The People of New
Mexico 69

Learning for
Life 71

Keeping Tradition
Alive 74

Modern
Art 76

New Mexican
Writers 77

Participants in a
cultural parade at
the New Mexico
State Fair

CHAPTER SIX

PEOPLE

★

NEW MEXICO'S CULTURE HAS BEEN LARGELY SHAPED BY FOUR GROUPS OF PEOPLE: Native Americans, Hispanics,* African Americans, and Anglos. Later arrivals from Asia and other parts of the world added to the mix, bringing their own traditions. New Mexico's population is small—it ranks 36th out of the 50 states—but growing. People come for jobs, warm weather, and to enjoy New Mexico's unique mix of cultures.

*For consistency within the America the Beautiful series of books, the editors chose to use the word Hispanics. But in New Mexico, people of Spanish descent refer to themselves as Hispanos.

66

Jumping rope in Las Cruces

Big City Life

This list shows the population of New Mexico's biggest cities.

Albuquerque 504,949
Las Cruces 86,268
Santa Fe 72,056
Rio Rancho 71,607
Roswell 45,582

Source: U.S. Census Bureau, 2006 estimates

CITIES, VILLAGES, NATIONS

Albuquerque, with more than 500,000 people, is the largest city in New Mexico. About one-quarter of the state's population calls the city home, and tens of thousands more live in the surrounding suburbs. As a center for business, arts, and education, Albuquerque buzzes with activity. Yet the city is near many natural wonders and open spaces, so people can easily take a break from city life.

Sizable cities, such as Santa Fe, Las Cruces, Gallup, and Rio Rancho, are scattered around the state. But small towns and villages are more common. Some are nestled high in the mountains. Others consist of nothing more than a few buildings that dot the high desert. Satellite dishes help bring the Internet and television to these remote areas. But many rural residents enjoy being far from the hustle and bustle of city life.

Where New Mexicans Live

The colors on this map indicate population density throughout the state. The darker the color, the more people live there.

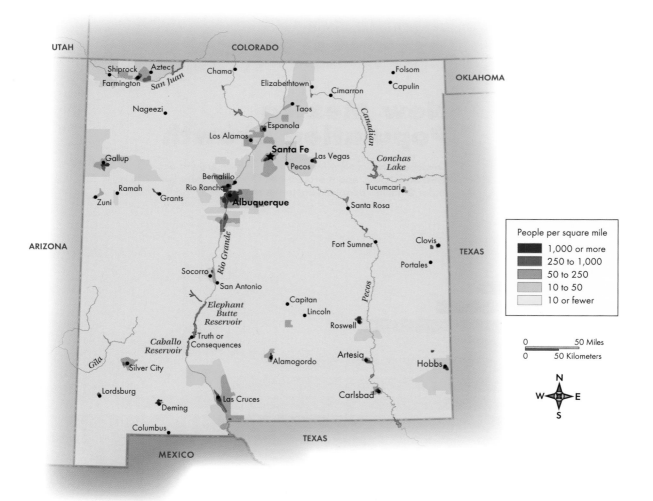

Although New Mexico is a state, it is also home to several dozen "nations." Each Native American pueblo and reservation is considered a nation, with its own leaders and laws. Some Native Americans choose to live outside Native lands and return only for special events. Those who remain on Native lands pursue a variety of lifestyles. Many people live completely modern lives, commuting to and from jobs, and embracing the latest technology. But at the ancient village of Taos Pueblo, people live as their ancestors did hundreds of years ago. They have no electricity, and they still bake bread in traditional adobe ovens.

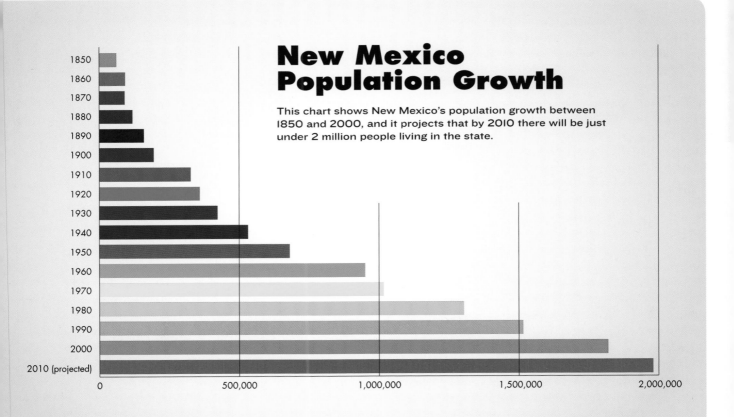

New Mexico Population Growth

This chart shows New Mexico's population growth between 1850 and 2000, and it projects that by 2010 there will be just under 2 million people living in the state.

This Navajo woman raises sheep, spins their wool, and weaves it into rugs.

THE PEOPLE OF NEW MEXICO

Saying that New Mexico is a mix of Native American, Hispanic, African American, and Anglo cultures doesn't paint a full picture of the state. Within each group, there are distinct differences. The Native Americans include the 19 Pueblo tribes, two groups of Apaches, the Navajos, and Native Americans who moved from the Great Plains. Even some of the Pueblo groups are distinct: three different languages are spoken at the pueblos.

The Hispanics of New Mexico include families who trace their roots to the first Spanish settlers, as well as recent arrivals from Mexico and Central America. Anglos include people from many European back-

MINI-BIO

N. SCOTT MOMADAY: THE INDIAN EXPERIENCE

N. Scott Momaday (1934–), a Kiowa from Oklahoma, spent much of his youth at Jemez Pueblo. For a time, he also lived on Apache and Navajo reservations. As an adult, he explored his Native American background in words. In 1968, he published his first novel, *House Made of Dawn*. The book won a Pulitzer Prize, a major award for U.S. writers. His other writings include poems, stories, and articles about Native American history. Momaday believes living among Indians from different nations was a good experience: "We didn't have the same language, but I always had a sense of being one of them because I'm Indian. . . . We got along well because we were all Indians together."

? Want to know more? See www.english.uiuc.edu/maps/poets/m_r/momaday/momaday.htm

grounds. Some came from the eastern United States. Others came from Ireland, Italy, and eastern Europe. More recently, people have arrived from Germany and Canada. A growing number of Asians are also settling in New Mexico, particularly in Albuquerque and other cities. The African American population has been growing since 1970, now making up 2.4 percent of the state's population. Some can trace their roots to the Buffalo Soldiers or workers who came west to build railroads.

People QuickFacts

Persons of Hispanic or Latino origin: 43.4%[†]

White persons not Hispanic: 43.1%

American Indian and Alaska Native persons: 10.2%[*]

Black persons: 2.4%[*]

Asian persons: 1.3%[*]

Native Hawaiian and Other Pacific Islander: 0.1%[*]

Persons reporting two or more races: 1.5%

[†]Includes persons reporting only one race
[*]Hispanics may be of any race, so they also are included in applicable race categories
Source: U.S. Census Bureau, 2005 estimate

A student works in a laboratory at the University of New Mexico in Albuquerque.

LEARNING FOR LIFE

New Mexicans were slow to build public schools, and for centuries the Catholic Church educated the young. Today, public, private, and religious schools all give students the learning they need to succeed in life. The state is making an extra effort to improve education among Native Americans. This includes teaching students their native language in addition to English.

Students who go on to college have many choices if they stay in the state. The largest school is the University of New Mexico in Albuquerque, with branches in Gallup, Los Alamos, Taos, and Valencia. The school is well known for its work in Latin American history and the history of the American West. Other important state-run schools are New Mexico State University in Las Cruces, the New Mexico Institute of Mining and Technology in Socorro, and Highlands University in Las Vegas. New Mexico also has several small private colleges, including St. John's College in Santa Fe.

HOW TO TALK LIKE A NEW MEXICAN

To talk like a New Mexican, you might want to know a few words of Spanish. Drive through most New Mexican neighborhoods and you're sure to see large red chile peppers tied to a string. That long tail of peppers is called a *ristra*. One term from Caló (Mexican Spanish slang) is *nel, pastel,* which means "no way" (literally "no cake"). But New Mexico has a cowboy heritage, too. Cowboys and cowgirls might call an outspoken person a "maverick," like an unbranded animal. When a rider is thrown from a horse, some say he is "tasting gravel."

HOW TO EAT LIKE A NEW MEXICAN

As with so much in New Mexico, what's for dinner can include something Spanish, Anglo, Indian—or all three! Other immigrants brought food ranging from egg rolls to pizza.

Perhaps the one food most connected to New Mexico is the chile pepper. Spanish settlers brought the first chiles with them from Mexico. To the rest of the United States, they're "chili" peppers, but you'd better change that last "i" to an "e" in New Mexico. Local residents insist that the traditional Spanish spelling, "chile," be used. Many peppers are green when they're picked, but they turn shades of red as they dry in the sun.

FAQ ★ ★ ★

Q8 WHAT DOES "RED OR GREEN?" MEAN IN A RESTAURANT?

A8 "Red or green?" is the official state question in New Mexico. It means, "Do you want red chile sauce or green chile sauce with your food?" People who can't decide sometimes answer "Christmas," which means a little bit of both.

Hot chile peppers

MENU

WHAT'S ON THE MENU IN NEW MEXICO?

Sopaipilla

The New Mexican sopaipilla is a creation that likely dates back to colonial Albuquerque. A thin square of wheat flour is fried in oil. While it cooks, it puffs up like a small, hollow pillow. Some people put meat, cheese, or peppers inside. Others cover the treat with honey.

Posole

This stew features corn, pork, and chiles, all cooked together for several hours. In southern New Mexico, only red chiles are used, but northerners sometimes use green instead. In any color, posole makes a hearty meal, and it's often a favorite on Christmas Eve.

"Cowboy" Food

Long ago, cowboys cooked potatoes, beans, and meat over open flames while they moved cattle across the plains. Those foods are still part of many New Mexican meals.

Piñon

Piñon pine trees grow in New Mexico's mountains. Their nuts turn up in all sorts of recipes in New Mexico, from breads to candy. Some say the best way to eat these pine nuts is roasted.

TRY THIS RECIPE
Red Chile Sauce

New Mexicans know something about chile peppers—they've grown them for more than 400 years. Here's a recipe for one of New Mexico's favorite foods, a sauce you can use to spice up tacos, enchiladas, and anything else that seems a little bland. Have an adult help you with this recipe.

Ingredients:
10 to 12 dried red chiles
1 medium onion, chopped
2 cloves garlic, chopped
2 tablespoons vegetable oil
1 cup water

Instructions:
1. Split open the chiles and remove the stems and seeds. (Be sure not to touch your eyes after working with the chiles—it will hurt!) Rinse off the chiles and place them in a pot. Cover them with hot water. Let the chiles sit for 15 minutes and then remove them from the water. You can save some of the water to use in step 3.
2. Sauté the onion and garlic in the oil until they are soft, about 5 minutes.
3. Place all the ingredients and the cup of water into a blender or food processor. Mix until you have a fiery red sauce!

Piñon nuts

MINI-BIO

MARIA MARTINEZ: MASTER POTTER

Maria Martinez (1887—1980) made Pueblo pottery a widely admired art form. She was born at San Ildefonso, where she learned pottery from her aunt. Martinez demonstrated her work at the St. Louis World's Fair in 1904. By 1919, she had developed her famous black on black pottery, in which black designs are set on a shiny black background. She also did something other Native American potters had not— she signed her name on her work. Soon her work was winning prizes and commanding high prices. Her husband, Julian, painted the designs on many of her pieces. Together, they taught their style to their children. Members of the Martinez family still make black on black pottery.

? Want to know more? See http://taosartschool.org/ maria_martinez/martinez.htm

KEEPING TRADITION ALIVE

For centuries, the Pueblo have made pottery, baskets, jewelry, and weavings. The items were meant for daily use, but they were also artistic creations. These skills have been passed down, and Native Americans in New Mexico today continue the artistic traditions.

Each Pueblo has its own style of pottery. At Taos, some potters still shape their work by hand, while Native Americans elsewhere use a turning wheel to help shape their creations.

A jeweler in his workshop at the Santo Domingo Pueblo

GEORGE LÓPEZ: A CARVER'S CRAFT

As a boy, George López (1900—1993) watched his father, José, carve santos out of aspen wood. The family lived in Córdova, a small town near the Sangre de Cristo Mountains. Carvers in this remote area had kept alive the craft of woodcarving, which dates back to the 18th century. George (seen here with his wife, Sabinita) became a carver, too. He was well known for his unpainted santos, carrying on the style he learned from his father. Today, other members of the López family continue to work as santeros.

? Want to know more? See www.nea.gov/honors/heritage/fellows/fellow.php?id=1982_05

Navajo rugs for sale in Santa Fe

Some Jemez potters paint animals on their work, and certain potters of San Ildefonso specialize in making black pottery. Collectors pay thousands of dollars for the work of the best Pueblo artists. Weaving is a specialty of the Navajos. Navajo rugs and blankets are prized the world over for their designs, which often feature zigzag lines and geometric shapes. Native Americans in New Mexico also make jewelry. They often work in silver and turquoise.

The Spanish settlers also had their crafts, which have endured. In colonial days, carvers made statues and wooden screens that showed saints or people from the Bible. The general name for these is *santos*—"saints"—and the artists are called *santeros*. Today, New Mexico's santeros carve both religious items and images from everyday life.

GEORGIA O'KEEFFE: PAINTER OF THE DESERT

Wisconsin native Georgia O'Keeffe (1887–1986) made her first long visit to New Mexico in 1929 and fell in love with its scenery and light. She returned each summer for several years. Then, in 1940, she bought an adobe house near Abiquiu, west of Taos. She knocked down some of its walls and put in glass, to make it easier to paint her surroundings. She collected animal bones in the desert, which also appeared in her work. Some art historians consider O'Keeffe one of the world's great painters, and her images of New Mexico are among her best works.

Want to know more? See www.okeeffemuseum.org/background/index.html

Ernest Blumenschein seated in front of his painting *The Extraordinary Affray* in 1927

MODERN ART

Anglo artists brought modern painting styles to New Mexico. Georgia O'Keeffe is the best-known for her paintings of flowers, cattle bones, and landscapes. Another is Ernest Blumenschein, who helped make Taos a center for art. He was known for painting the scenery and people he saw around him. Native-born artists include Peter Hurd, who also painted images of Western scenery, and R. C. Gorman, a Navajo, who won fame for his colorful images of Navajo women. Chiricahua Apache sculptor Allan Houser studied in Santa Fe before becoming famous for his works in wood, bronze, and stone. Anglo sculptor Glenna Goodacre has a studio in Santa Fe. Her work includes the image of the Shoshone guide Sacagawea that is found on U.S. dollar coins.

A MUSICAL LAND

Music has filled the air of New Mexico for several thousand years. The Anasazis used drums and dance in their ceremonies, and so do today's Native people. Tom Bee, originally from Gallup, is perhaps the best-known Indian musician in the state. For more than 30 years, he has written, played, and produced Native American music. At times he blends traditional styles with modern rock and pop. Mariachi music, which originated in Mexico, is also popular in New Mexico. Mariachi bands usually include several guitars, violins, and a trumpet. They often play at weddings. Like mariachi music, folk dancing called *folklorico* traces its roots to Mexico and is popular among the Hispanic residents of New Mexico.

Taos drums

NEW MEXICAN WRITERS

Tony Hillerman is a popular novelist who writes detective stories featuring two Navajos as the heroes. Poet and scholar Luci Tapahonso is from Shiprock. She often writes in her native Navajo language. Rudolfo Anaya first won fame with his novel *Bless Me, Ultima*, the story of a Hispanic teen living in a small New Mexico town. He has also written several children's books,

Writer Rudolfo Anaya at a book signing in Albuquerque

Folk dancers perform at the annual Tularosa Fiesta.

including *The Farolitos of Christmas*, which describes the New Mexican tradition of lighting *farolitos* (lanterns).

ON THE BALL

New Mexico doesn't have any major professional sports teams, but that doesn't mean folks don't have something to cheer about. Albuquerque is home to a minor league baseball team called the Isotopes. The Isotopes' home field also hosts the annual Native American All-

Star Game, which features players from Pueblo teams.

The University of New Mexico, Albuquerque, has a number of outstanding sports teams, nicknamed The Lobos. Its men's soccer team is usually ranked as one of the best in the country. The women's basketball program is also highly ranked, and the football team has sent several players to the pros. The best-known is New Mexico native Brian Urlacher, one of the top linebackers in the National Football League. New Mexico State also has a successful college sports program.

New Mexicans have played a big part in two sports that couldn't be more different: auto racing and ballooning. The Unser family of Albuquerque has produced several top race-car drivers. Al Unser, brother Bobby, and Al's son Al Jr. have a total of nine wins at the Indianapolis 500, one of the world's most famous races. Traveling at a much slower speed, balloonists compete in Albuquerque's yearly fiesta. Balloonists try to fly the farthest distance, land in certain areas, or race to reach a target before the other balloons. In 1978, New Mexico balloonists Maxie Anderson, Ben Abruzzo, and Larry Newman made the world's first balloon trip across the Atlantic Ocean.

New Mexicans from all walks of life are making their mark. And they know that their state is a great place to call home.

NANCY LOPEZ: GREAT GOLFER

Champion golfer Nancy Lopez (1957–) perfected her game as a young girl in Roswell. At 12, she was the top women's golfer in the state. At Goddard High School in Roswell, she played for the boy's team. Few high schools in the United States had many sports teams for girls at that time. Lopez's precise drives and putts made the team state champions. In 1978, she began playing professionally. During her career, she won 48 tournaments.

Want to know more? Go to: www.lpga.com/player_results.aspx?id=500

READ ABOUT

The Center
of State
Government...82

The Legislative
Branch 84

The Executive
Branch 86

The Judicial
Branch 86

Government
Closer to
Home.......89

Governor Bill
Richardson greets
students visiting
the state capitol.

CHAPTER SEVEN

GOVERNMENT

★

I N 2006, JORDAN MCKITTRICK WAS A 15-YEAR-OLD STUDENT IN SANTA FE. He met two survivors of World War II and developed an interest in ending wars. So he and eight other New Mexicans visited U.S. senator Pete Domenici. The group wanted the senator to seek a quick end to the war in Iraq. Some New Mexicans like Jordan oppose the war. Others support it, and thousands of New Mexicans serve in the military. New Mexicans differ on many issues, and they count on their leaders to balance opposing views when they make decisions for the state.

The state capitol in Santa Fe

THE CENTER OF STATE GOVERNMENT

Santa Fe has served as the capital of New Mexico, first as part of New Spain, then as part of Mexico, and finally as one of the United States. Today, New Mexico lawmakers meet at the state capitol, which is known as the Roundhouse. The governor and lieutenant governor have offices there. The state's supreme

Capitol Facts

Here are some facts about New Mexico's state capitol.

Number of stories . . . . 3, plus one level belowground
Diameter of dome . . . . 24.5 feet (7.5 m)
Height of dome . . . . 60 feet (18 m)
Opened 1966
Cost of construction . . . . $4.7 million

Capital City

This map shows places of interest around Santa Fe, New Mexico's capital city.

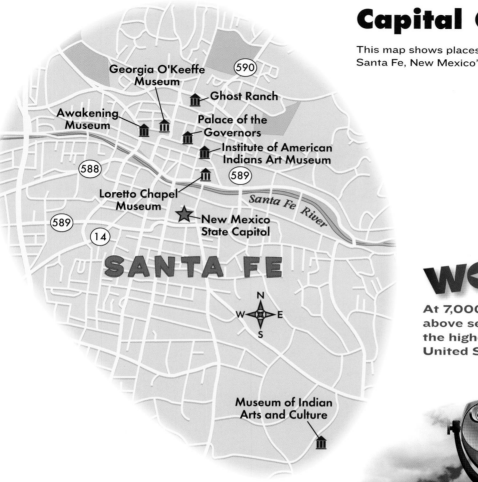

Georgia O'Keeffe Museum

Ghost Ranch

Awakening Museum

Palace of the Governors

Institute of American Indians Art Museum

Loretto Chapel Museum

New Mexico State Capitol

SANTA FE

Museum of Indian Arts and Culture

Santa Fe River

At 7,000 feet (2,100 m) above sea level, Santa Fe is the highest capital city in the United States.

court meets in Santa Fe in its own building not far from the Roundhouse. This building opened in 1937.

New Mexico's government, like the federal government, has three branches. The legislative branch makes laws, the executive branch carries out the laws (and often proposes new ones), and the judicial branch makes sure the laws are carried out fairly.

SEE IT HERE!

THE ROUNDHOUSE

The Roundhouse is the only round capitol in the United States. Built partly in a Pueblo adobe style, the Roundhouse has four short wings jutting out at equal points around the circle. From above, the building looks a little like the Zia Pueblo sun symbol, which is shown on New Mexico's state flag. The Roundhouse is the fourth building in Santa Fe to have served as the capitol of New Mexico. The first capitol building was the historic Palace of the Governors, which is now a museum of New Mexican history.

Jose Bremer, the Mexican ambassador to the United States, addresses a joint session of the New Mexico legislature.

Representing New Mexico

This list shows the number of elected officials who represent New Mexico, both on the state and national levels.

OFFICE	NUMBER	LENGTH OF TERM
State senators	42	4 years
State representatives	70	2 years
U.S. senators	2	6 years
U.S. representatives	3	2 years
Presidential electors	5	—

THE LEGISLATIVE BRANCH

New Mexico lawmakers form the state legislature, which includes the house of representatives and the senate. The representatives and senators present bills (proposals for new laws). The bills are debated and then voted on by both the house and the senate. Both parts of the legislature must approve a bill before it is sent to the governor, who decides whether or not the bill will become law.

The legislature tackles all sorts of problems. Entering the 21st century, New Mexico's students often did not perform as well as students in other states. In response, lawmakers wrote bills that called for taxpayer-funded prekindergarten classes across New Mexico.

Voters also have a say in the lawmaking process. They can try to get rid of a law through a process that is called referendum. After enough people sign a **petition**, voters can decide whether or not the law stays on the law books.

MINI-BIO

BILL RICHARDSON: NEW MEXICO'S DIPLOMAT

Bill Richardson (1947–) was well known before he became New Mexico's governor in 2002. The son of a Mexican mother and an Anglo father, he became interested in politics and government during college. He settled in Santa Fe in 1978 and four years later was elected to the U.S. House of Representatives. During the 1990s, President Bill Clinton named Richardson to several important posts, including U.S. ambassador to the United Nations. Richardson showed a skill for easing international conflicts. In 2006, while governor of New Mexico, he helped win the release of an American kidnapped in the African country of Sudan.

? Want to know more? See www.governor. state.nm.us/index2.php

WEIRD LAWS

Every state has laws that can seem a little wacky, and New Mexico is no different. Here are a few:
In Raton, women better watch what they wear before getting on a horse. Riding while in a Japanese robe called a kimono is a no-no! The town of Carlsbad forbids the use of *Merriam-Webster's Collegiate Dictionary*. Put away your hunting rifle if you go to Deming's Mountain View Cemetery—it's illegal to hunt there. Deming also won't let you lead an animal along the town's sidewalks.

WORD TO KNOW

petition *a list of voters' signatures requesting some action*

86

OCTAVIANO LARRAZOLO: POLITICAL LEADER

When New Mexico was a U.S. territory, all but one of its governors were Anglo. After New Mexico became a state, voters chose Octaviano Larrazolo (1859–1930) as their first Hispanic governor in 1919. Larrazolo was born in Mexico, but settled in New Mexico in 1895. He worked as a teacher and a lawyer before entering politics. During the 1920s, he served in the New Mexico state legislature. Then, in 1928, he became the first Hispanic to sit in the U.S. Senate. Illness forced him to leave that post after only a few months.

? Want to know more? See www.loc.gov/rr/hispanic/congress/larrazolo.html

The New Mexico commissioner of public lands manages some 13 million acres (5 million hectares) of land with valuable natural resources. That's an area about the size of Massachusetts and Vermont combined.

THE EXECUTIVE BRANCH

The governor is one of seven executive branch positions elected by New Mexicans. The governor is the leader of the executive branch and chooses people to lead various departments. The legislature must approve these choices. The governor also signs bills into law and proposes the state budget. The state lawmakers, however, have the final say on how much money is spent and where it goes.

The lieutenant governor of New Mexico steps in to lead the executive branch if the governor is out of the state or otherwise can't serve. Other executive branch offices include secretary of state, attorney general, treasurer, and auditor. The commissioner of public lands watches over the money the state makes from its natural resources. These include oil, natural gas, and minerals. Most of the money earned from these resources goes to the state's schools.

THE JUDICIAL BRANCH

Finding plenty of water is tough for many New Mexico communities. For decades, a town could use as much water as it wanted from local sources, even if that meant there was little water left for other towns. In 2004, however, the state supreme court overturned this rule, which traced its roots back to colonial days.

The state supreme court is just one part of New Mexico's judicial branch. In most cases, voters choose

New Mexico's State Government

EXECUTIVE BRANCH
Carries out state laws

Governor

Lieutenant Governor

Secretary of State

Attorney General

Treasurer

Auditor

LEGISLATIVE BRANCH
Makes and passes state laws

Senate (42 members)

House of Representatives (70 members)

JUDICIAL BRANCH
Enforces state laws

Supreme Court

Court of Appeals

District Court (13)

Magistrate Court (54)

Municipal Court (80)

Probate Court (33)

the judges who serve in the judiciary. Municipal courts deal with people who break local laws. Magistrate courts handle cases involving small debts or legal claims. The state's 13 district courts hear cases appealed from these lower courts. They also handle criminal cases and larger civil suits. If someone thinks a district court made an error, he or she can ask the seven judges on the court of appeals to review the case.

The most powerful court in New Mexico is the supreme court. Its five judges, called justices, serve eight-year terms. The supreme court hears cases from the lower courts. It also decides if laws follow New Mexico's **constitution**.

WORD TO KNOW

constitution *a written document that contains all the governing principles of a state or country*

New Mexico Counties

This map shows the 33 counties in New Mexico. Santa Fe, the state capital, is indicated with a star.

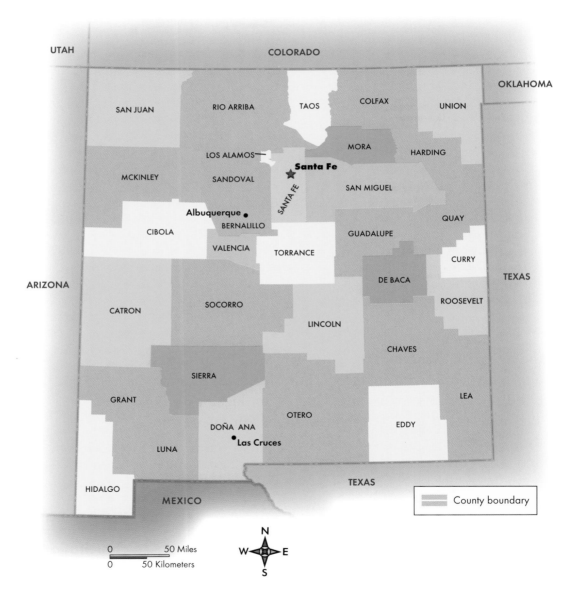

GOVERNMENT CLOSER TO HOME

New Mexico is divided into 33 counties, each with its own government. Voters elect county commissioners, who act as both a mini-legislature and executives. Voters also elect a treasurer, sheriff, assessor, probate judge, and clerk. A county manager helps carry out the commission's policies. Within each county are various cities, towns, and villages. Local and county governments build schools and libraries, hire police officers, and provide other essential public services.

New Mexico also has another kind of local government. By U.S. law, each Native American tribe is considered an independent nation. Voters on each pueblo and reservation choose a tribal president and council. These officials make business decisions for the nations and provide essential services. New Mexico's Indian Affairs Department works with the tribal governments to provide services the tribes can't afford on their own, such as building roads or stringing up power lines in remote areas. As U.S. citizens, Native Americans can vote in all state and national elections.

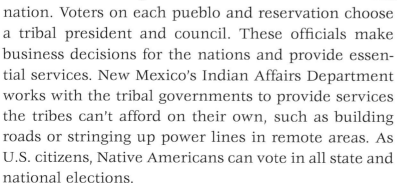

MINI-BIO

JOE GARCIA: RECLAIMING A NAME

For years, Joe Garcia (1953–) worked as an engineer at New Mexico's Los Alamos National Laboratory. A member of the San Juan Pueblo, he became involved in village politics in 1991. He first served as lieutenant governor and then became governor in 1995. Ten years later, he was governor for a second term when he made an important announcement for his people. The pueblo wanted to be known by its original name: Ohkay Owingeh. This Tewa language phrase means "place of strong people." San Juan was the name Spanish explorer Juan de Oñate had given the pueblo almost 400 years before. In 2005, Garcia was elected to head the National Congress of American Indians, the oldest tribal group in the United States.

? Want to know more? See www.doleta.gov/dinap/cfml/cncldir.cfm#JoeGarcia

State Flag

The first flag for New Mexico showed a small U.S. flag in one corner, the state seal in another, and the words *New Mexico*, all on a blue background. In 1920, some New Mexicans called for a new flag that would reflect the state's history. The resulting flag, introduced in 1925, is still used today. It shows a modern version of an old Zia symbol for the sun, with red rays pointing in four directions. The Zias considered the number four holy, because so many things come in fours—the main directions on a compass, the four seasons, and the four main stages of a person's life: childhood, youth, adulthood, and old age.

State Seal

New Mexico's first official seal was created after it became a U.S. territory in 1851. This seal showed an American eagle holding an olive branch in one claw and three arrows in the other. About 10 years later, a new seal showed a bald eagle with its wings outstretched. Underneath the wings was a smaller Mexican eagle holding a snake in its beak. In its claw was a cactus. In 1882, a small banner was placed beneath the eagles. It carries the Latin phrase *Crescit Eundo*, which means "It grows as it goes." Those words became the state's motto after it joined the Union in 1912, and the territorial seal became the state seal in 1913.

READ ABOUT

Farming and Ranching 94

Wealth from the Earth 98

Making Great Things 99

Looking to the Skies 99

Services of All Kinds 100

A worker at the Shidoni Foundry in Santa Fe, a company known for its high-quality bronze

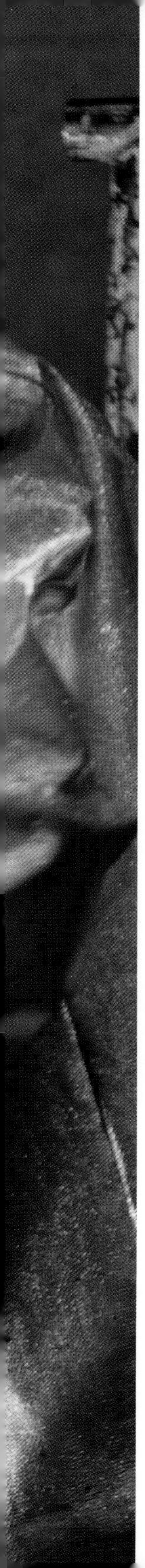

CHAPTER EIGHT

ECONOMY

ECONOMY ECONOMY ECONOM

IN COLONIAL DAYS, MOST NEW MEXICANS WERE FARMERS. Today, some people still grow crops and raise sheep and cattle. But most New Mexicans work in other jobs. Some spend their days in gleaming labs researching and developing new products. Others build high-tech gadgets in modern factories. Some mine the earth, while others drill for oil and gas. And a large number of New Mexicans make sure the state's many visitors have a good time exploring the Land of Enchantment!

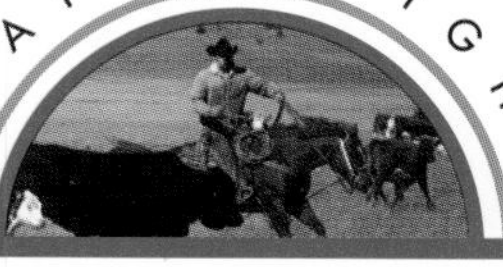

A cowboy rounds up cattle at Diamond Ranch.

FARMING AND RANCHING

Almost 60 percent of the state's land is used for agriculture, and the biggest chunk of that is used for ranching. Raising cattle is big business in New Mexico, just as it was in the Old West. Cattle and dairy products are the state's top agricultural items. Many sheep are also raised in the state. The wool of the churro sheep is prized for its strength.

What Do New Mexicans Do?

This color-coded chart shows what industries
New Mexicans work in.

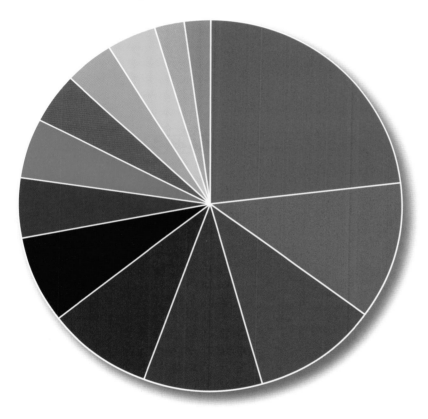

23.1% Educational services, health care,
and social assistance, 196,405

11.9% Retail trade, 101,023

10.7% Professional, scientific,
management, administrative,
and waste management services,
91,439

10.0% Arts, entertainment, recreation,
accommodation, and food services,
84,690

8.9% Construction, 75,400

7.5% Public administration, 63,543

5.3% Finance, insurance, real estate,
rental, and leasing, 44,894

5.3% Manufacturing, 45,305

4.5% Other services, except public
administration, 38,660

4.1% Agriculture, forestry, fishing,
hunting, and mining, 34,725

4.1% Transportation, warehousing, and
utilities, 35,080

2.6% Wholesale trade, 22,439

2.0% Information, 17,218

Source: U.S. Census Bureau, 2005 estimate

New Mexico's top crops are hay, plants and flowers, and nuts. The nuts grown include pecans, pistachios, and piñons. Other important farm products are cotton and vegetables. The Anasazis grew cotton centuries ago, and today New Mexican farmers sell about $25 million worth of cotton every year. The most famous New Mexican vegetables are chiles. They come in different sizes and spiciness—from mild to mouth-burning!

SEE IT HERE!

GO NUTS!

Pistachio trees grow best in a desert climate, making them perfect for New Mexico. The Eagle Ranch, in Alamogordo, offers free tours to show how nuts are harvested from the trees and then prepared for market. When pistachio nuts are ripe, a good shake of the branch will send them falling to the ground. At Eagle Ranch, they sell the nuts plain, salted, or dusted with red chile powder. That's one spicy snack!

MINI-BIO

ROY NAKAYAMA: THE CHILE MAN

Roy Nakayama (1923–1988) grew up on a farm in the Mesilla Valley of New Mexico. He stayed in the state almost his entire life and helped make the chile pepper a popular vegetable. Working as a plant scientist at New Mexico State University, he created new types of peppers. In 1975, he came up with one he called NuMex Big Jim. The pepper was almost 8 inches (20 cm) long, and it won a place in the Guinness Book of World Records as the biggest pepper ever! Nakayama also bred peppers that weren't too spicy, making them popular with backyard gardeners. For his efforts, he was sometimes called "the chile man."

❓ **Want to know more?** See www.epcc.edu/nwlibrary/borderlands/09_men.htm

Major Agricultural and Mining Products

This map shows where New Mexico's major agricultural and mining products come from. See a red and black drop? That means oil is found there.

Legend:
- Beans
- Cattle
- Coal
- Copper
- Cotton
- Dairy
- Fruit
- Gold
- Grains
- Hay
- Lead
- Mineral mining
- Natural gas
- Nuts
- Oil
- Potatoes
- Sheep
- Silver
- Vegetables

- Urban area
- Forests, some farming
- Grazing, rangeland
- Farming

Top Products

Agriculture Dairy products, cattle, hay, pecans, greenhouse plants and flowers, cotton, onions, chiles

Manufacturing Food products, computers and electronics, transportation equipment

Mining Coal, natural gas, oil, copper, sand and gravel, potash, molybdenum

New Mexico leads the country in the production of potash, digging up more than 1 million tons in 2004. That's more than 85 percent of all the potash produced in the United States.

WEALTH FROM THE EARTH

Mining ores and removing other valuable resources from the ground keep tens of thousands of New Mexicans working. Coal, which is burned to create electricity, is the number-one mineral in New Mexico. The state also produces copper, potash (used to make glass, fertilizer, and some medicines), sand and gravel for construction, and molybdenum. Smaller amounts of gold and silver are also mined.

THINK ABOUT IT!

To Mine or Not to Mine?

PRO

Starting in the 1940s, companies came to New Mexico to mine uranium. The Navajo lands in northwestern New Mexico hold large amounts of the mineral. When prices for uranium fell, all of the mines closed. But now uranium is valuable again, and the mining companies want to return to New Mexico. Some leaders of Cibola County support mining. In September 2006, the leaders noted that the county was "blessed with natural resources such as uranium," and mining it would "provide a significant tax base and additional jobs for Cibola County."

CON

Some Navajos oppose reopening the mines on their lands. Uranium mining releases a form of energy called radiation into the water and the air. Radiation can be deadly in large doses. Navajo president Joseph Shirley said, "In times past, they've already killed many of us with their [coming] upon our lands to mine the ore."

Some 40,000 oil and gas wells are scattered across New Mexico. Only two states produce more gas, and only three have more oil in the ground. Most of New Mexico's oil is pumped in the southeast corner of the state, while gas is most plentiful in the northwest corner.

MAKING GREAT THINGS

New companies spring up, requiring offices or warehouses. People moving into the state need homes. More homes and more people mean more services are needed. This also means a boom for the construction industry.

New Mexico has taken part in the high-tech boom since the 1970s. Major advances in electronics, lasers, and other high-tech fields have come from the Sandia and Los Alamos National Laboratories. The University of New Mexico and other state schools also carry out important research in science and technology. Intel, a private company, makes the silicon chips that power computers. It has about 5,000 workers at its Rio Rancho plant north of Albuquerque. Many smaller companies also provide jobs making electronic devices.

LOOKING TO THE SKIES

A dry climate and open spaces drew rocket inventor Robert Goddard to New Mexico in the 1930s. Today, those same conditions help New Mexico attract jobs tied to **aviation** and spaceflight. The U.S. government performs research into rockets at the White Sands Missile Range. The government also has three air force bases in New Mexico. Together, they provide New Mexicans with tens of thousands of jobs. Near Socorro, the government operates the Very Large Array, a field of 27 huge satellite dishes. The satellites detect objects in space.

Q: WHAT IS MOLYBDENUM?

A: Molybdenum is a silvery metal. It's often mixed with steel and iron to make them stronger. New Mexico's major molybdenum mine is located near Taos. It produced more than 3 million pounds (1.4 million kg) of the mineral in 2005.

WORD TO KNOW

aviation *the design and manufacture of airplanes*

MINI-BIO

CHERYL WILLMAN: SEEKING A CURE

In her lab, Cheryl Willman (1955–) peers through microscopes and looks at test results. For more than 25 years, she has sought a cure for leukemia, a form of cancer. As a college student in Minnesota, she had thought about becoming a lawyer. But she turned to medicine because of her grandmother, who had wanted to be a doctor but never had the chance. Willman is now head of the Cancer Research and Treatment Center at the University of New Mexico. The work she and other doctors have done there has made the center one of the best in the country. She once saw patients on a regular basis. But as she said in 2006, "I felt that I could have a far greater impact on a greater number of people through research."

? Want to know more? See www.aaci-cancer.org/update/n_update3.asp?upid=12&ndate=10/1/2005

When Eclipse Aviation opened, New Mexico entered the field of aircraft manufacturing. In 2006, the company delivered its first jet. Each of Eclipse's planes carries six passengers and is intended for small businesses. The Eclipse jet is lighter and less costly than other planes its size.

Spaceport America takes passengers even higher in the sky. The port, being built in Upham, is the world's first center devoted to space travel for businesses and tourists. Spaceport's first successful launch was in 2007. The port is scheduled for completion by 2010, at which point "regular" people, not only trained astronauts, will be able to take rides into space.

SERVICES OF ALL KINDS

Banking, selling goods, government work, and health care are just some parts of New Mexico's service economy. When it comes to putting people to work, the government leads the way. More than 170,000 people work for some level of government—local, county, state, federal, or tribal. The U.S. government is the largest employer in the state, hiring about one out of every four workers.

Another service involves taking care of the more than 20 million tourists who visit New Mexico each year. Those guests spend almost $5 billion, keeping tour guides, chefs, hotel workers, and others in the tourism industry on their toes.

Visitors also spend money at New Mexico pueblos and reservations. Some visitors want to learn about Native American history. Some visit pueblo casinos, resort hotels, and golf courses. Tourism brings income to the Native nations.

Visitors enjoy a performance by Zuni Pueblo dancers at the Bandelier National Monument.

CONRAD HILTON: A HOTEL FAMILY

As a boy in San Antonio, New Mexico, Conrad Hilton (1887–1979) watched his parents turn their home into a small inn. Guests paid a dollar a night for a clean room and a meal. As a young man, Hilton went to Texas and bought a hotel. Soon he owned several more, and one that opened in 1925 was the first to carry his name. Starting in the 1950s, he built a chain of Hilton hotels across the United States and overseas. Today, the Hilton Hotels Corporation has business ties to thousands of hotels.

? Want to know more? See www.hrm.uh.edu/cnhc/ShowContent.asp?c=9293

UTAH

COLORADO

OK

Shiprock   Aztec   Chama   Folsom

Farmington   *San Juan*   Capulin

Elizabethtown   Cimarron

Nageezi   Taos   *Canadian*

Los Alamos   Santa Fe   *Conchas Lake*

Gallup   Pecos   Las Vegas

Bernalillo   Tucumcari

Grants   Rio Rancho   Sandia Peak

Albuquerque   Santa Rosa

Zuni   Ramah   40

Fort Sumner

Clovis

ARIZONA

Rio Grande   Geographic Center of New Mexico   Portales

TEXAS

25

Socorro

San Antonio

Capitan   *Pecos*

Lincoln

Elephant Butte Reservoir   Roswell

Caballo Reservoir   Truth or Consequences   Alamogordo   Artesia   Hobbs

Gila   Silver City   Carlsbad

Las Cruces

10   Deming

Columbus   TEXAS

MEXICO   N   50 Miles

W⊹E   0   50 Kilometers

S

25 — Interstate highway

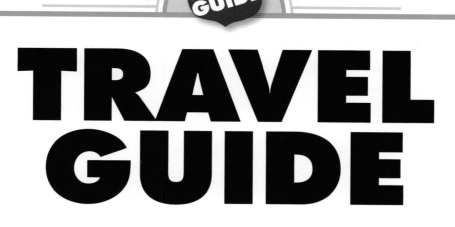

CHAPTER NINE

TRAVEL GUIDE

★

A LMOST ANYWHERE YOU LOOK IN NEW MEXICO, THERE'S SOME-THING FASCINATING TO SEE. The natural wonders include mountains, the remains of volcanoes, and beautiful rock formations. New Mexicans have built museums and attractions and spent money to improve their cities to cater to millions of visitors each year. Let's take a look at some of what New Mexico has to offer!

← Follow along with this travel map. We'll begin in Shiprock and travel all the way down to Carlsbad.

NORTH-WESTERN

THINGS TO DO: Explore Anasazi ruins, visit a city in the sky, and shiver in an ice cave.

Shiprock

★ **Shiprock:** The town and the rock share the same name. Some 19th-century soldiers thought the massive rock looked like a grand sailing ship, leading to the name. The Navajo believed Shiprock was once a giant bird. Scientists say the rock, which rises 1,800 feet (550 m) above the surrounding plain, is more than 12 million years old.

Shiprock

Nageezi

★ **Chaco Culture National Historical Park:** The most spectacular remains of the Anasazis in New Mexico are at Chaco Canyon. After bouncing over dirt roads, you come to the massive Pueblo Bonito and the rest of the ruins of what was once a great city. For a real adventure, walk the trails in remote parts of the park.

Aztec

★ **Aztec Ruins National Monument:** The pueblo here once had 500 rooms. A massive kiva at the site has been rebuilt for visitors to explore. Inside, you can hear recordings of Native American music.

Zuni

★ **Zuni Pueblo:** To the Spanish, the original Zuni pueblo was part of the legendary Seven Cities of Cíbola. Today, Zuni Pueblo is home to almost 12,000 people, making it the largest pueblo in New Mexico. The residents are happy to show you their art and some of their traditional dances.

The roof of the original Great Kiva at Aztec Ruins was thought to have weighed 90 tons.

SEE IT HERE!

SKY CITY

The people of Acoma didn't welcome the early Spanish explorers who wanted to enter their pueblo. But things have changed over the centuries, and now tourists can explore the "Sky City" of the Acomas. A van takes you up the 350-foot (107 m) mesa, where a tour guide explains Acoma history. The village includes a mission church from 1640. When the tour is over, you can leave the mesa using the same rocky stairway the Acomas have walked for centuries. The Acomas who still live in the Sky City have no electricity or running water.

Acoma pottery

Ramah

★ **El Morro National Monument:** A pool of water in the middle of desert country made El Morro a popular spot for travelers of old. Today, only animals drink from the pool, but visitors can see the words that humans carved into nearby rocks hundreds of years ago.

Grants

★ **Bandera Center/Ice Cave:** Here's a cool way to get some relief on a hot day—explore a cave of ice! A tube of hardened lava leads down to the cave, where the temperature never goes above 31°F (–1°C).

★ **El Malpais National Monument:** You'll see lava flows, ancient ruins, and historic homesteads at this site of prehistoric volcanoes.

La Ventana Natural Arch at El Malpais National Monument

NORTH-EASTERN NEW MEXICO

THINGS TO DO: Dive into the Blue Hole, stroll the streets where gunslingers once walked, and learn more about New Mexico's Rough Riders.

Las Vegas

★ **Rough Rider Memorial Collection and City of Las Vegas Museum:** The area around Las Vegas was home to many of the Rough Riders who served under Teddy Roosevelt during the Spanish-American War. The Rough Rider Memorial honors those brave New Mexicans and the future president who led them.

Cimarron

★ **Old Town:** Walk past the original buildings in the heart of Cimarron and you can almost smell the gunpowder and horses. A walking tour here includes Schwenk's Hall (a former hot spot for gambling), the St. James Hotel (where Wild West figures such as Jesse James and Buffalo Bill Cody stayed), and the Old Jail.

Scuba school at the Blue Hole

Santa Rosa

★ **Blue Hole:** It's hard to believe, but you can find a scuba-diving paradise in the middle of this dry state. The Blue Hole is 80 feet (24 m) deep and carved out of sandstone. The crystal-clear waters are 60°F (16°C) all year.

★ **Vermejo Park Ranch:** Covering an area almost as big as Rhode Island, this ranch is owned by Ted Turner, founder of Cable News Network (CNN). Guests come to see bear, bison, and other animals living in the wild.

Capulin

★ **Capulin Volcano National Monument:** Ever wanted to walk inside a volcano? Then head to Capulin. The volcano here erupted about 60,000 years ago. It's extinct now, so you can safely explore inside the volcano and walk along its rim.

NORTH-CENTRAL NEW MEXICO

THINGS TO DO: Explore ancient ruins, soar over Albuquerque, and learn about Hispanic culture.

Albuquerque

★ **Museum of Natural History and Science:** At the museum, you can explore more than 4 billion years of New Mexico history. As you enter, say hello to Spike and Alberta, dinosaur skeletons that stand on either side of the door. Inside, you can learn more about volcanoes and explore the stars in the museum's planetarium.

Museum of Natural History and Science

An art exhibit at the National Hispanic Cultural Center

★ **The National Hispanic Cultural Center:** Located in a traditionally Hispanic neighborhood, the cultural center promotes the study of everything Hispanic. It features art exhibits, musical performances, talks on Spanish-language literature, and Spanish language lessons.

★ **Indian Pueblo Cultural Center:** The 19 Pueblo groups of New Mexico own and operate this center, which features historic as well as contemporary art and **artifacts** from the pueblos.

WORD TO KNOW

artifacts *items created by humans, usually for a practical purpose*

MILLIE SANTILLANES: PRESERVING THE PAST

Through her mother's family, Millie Santillanes (1932–2007) had ties to some of Albuquerque's oldest Spanish families. Fiercely proud of that heritage, she worked hard to honor it. Starting in the 1960s, she ran several small businesses in the Old Town section of Albuquerque. She helped make that neighborhood a center for Spanish history and culture in the capital, and she later founded the New Mexican Hispanic Culture Preservation League. She also played a large role in organizing the celebration for the 300th anniversary of the city in 2006. Santillanes offended some people, who thought she ignored the cruelty of the early Spaniards toward the Pueblos. But her efforts to bring life to Old Town won her many local honors.

? Want to know more? See www.nmhcpl.org/Remembering_Millie_Santilla.html

★ **Petroglyph National Monument:** This site on the western edge of Albuquerque offers a glimpse into the Pueblos' past. Here, Native Americans left thousands of carvings in the rocks, some made more than 4,000 years ago.

Hikers at Sandia Peak

★ **Sandia Peak:** Located just northeast of Albuquerque, Sandia Peak is a 10,678-foot (3,255 m) mountain that's popular with skiers and snowboarders. Tourists can go partway up the mountain on a **tram** for a bird's-eye view of the region.

WORD TO KNOW

tram *a carrier that travels on overhead rails or cables*

Taos

★ **Taos Pueblo:** The pueblo has been continually occupied for at least 700 years, making it the oldest community in the United States. Here visitors can learn about Pueblo history. They can also buy goods from potters and other artists.

★ **Kit Carson Home and Museum:** The one-time frontier scout bought this home near the Taos Plaza as a wedding gift for his wife. Now you can walk the same wooden floors that Kit and his family used. Two other homes nearby serve as the museum, which offers a glimpse into Taos's past.

Taos Ski Valley

★ **Taos Ski Valley:** If gliding down powdery slopes is your thing, Taos Ski Valley is a must-see. Located about 20 miles (30 km) outside of Taos, the ski area has some of the toughest trails in the country. Snowboarders, though, are out of luck—Taos Ski Valley is just for skiers.

Chama

★ **The Cumbres and Toltec Scenic Railroad:** All aboard! A 1920s steam train takes visitors over the same route once used to haul silver and other minerals through the Rocky Mountains. The railroad is a "movie star," too—a dozen films have scenes that were shot along the mountain route!

Taos Pueblo

Santa Fe

★ **The Palace of the Governors:**
Spanish, Mexican, and American
officials have all worked within the
adobe walls of the Palace of the
Governors. Now it features exhibits on New Mexico's multicultural
past. Its courtyard is the scene of
performances and private parties,
and outside, facing the plaza, Indian
artists offer their goods for sale.

★ **Georgia O'Keeffe Museum:**
Just next door to the Palace of
the Governors is a museum dedicated to one of America's finest
painters, Georgia O'Keeffe. The
museum owns some of O'Keeffe's
best-known works and also displays items on loan from other art
collections.

Spiral staircase at Loretto Chapel

★ **Loretto Chapel:** A mystery swirls
around the spiral staircase that
makes this 1873 chapel unique. The
stairs make two full turns as they go
up, and nothing supports them. The
staircase is held together without
any screws or nails. Legends say a
saint built it, but others believe the
staircase is simply the work of a
very skilled carpenter.

★ **Museum Hill:** Four museums sit
on this spot, just southeast of the
center of Santa Fe. The Museum
of International Folk Art displays
work from more than 100 coun-
tries. The art and history of New

Native American crafts for sale at the Palace
of the Governors

Mexico's Native people is featured at the Museum of Indian Arts and Culture. The Wheelwright Museum of the American Indian has modern Native American art from across the Southwest. And the Museum of Spanish Colonial Art, the newest museum on the hill, shows the skills of the Spanish-speaking settlers who lived in New Mexico during the 18th and 19th centuries.

★ **The Roundhouse:** A trip to the Roundhouse lets you see how government operates in New Mexico. The state capitol has self-guided tours, and its beautiful grounds feature more than 100 kinds of plants and trees.

SEE IT HERE!

EL RANCHO DE LAS GOLONDRINAS

To step back in time to colonial New Mexico, head out of Santa Fe to this ranch. It is a "living" museum with actual buildings from 18th-century farms. Some have always been on the site, while others were moved there from elsewhere in northern New Mexico. Actors dressed in period clothes show how settlers lived on the frontier of colonial Spain.

Los Alamos

★ **Bandelier National Monument:** Climb into cliff dwellings that were once the home of Pueblo people at Bandelier. The site also has pueblo ruins and more than 70 miles (110 km) of hiking trails.

★ **Bradbury Science Museum:** You can't visit the labs at the Los Alamos National Laboratory, but you can learn a little about what goes on there at its science museum. Located in downtown Los Alamos, the Bradbury has exhibits on nuclear weapons, lasers, and high-tech wonders.

The Bradbury Science Museum

Pecos

★ **Pecos National Historical Park:** As many as 2,000 Pueblo people once lived here. When the Spanish came, they built a large mission church. Ruins from both the Pueblo and the Spanish are yours to explore.

A satellite dish in the Very Large Array

SOUTH-WESTERN

THINGS TO DO: Take a refreshing dip in the hot springs, learn about some very large "dishes" in Socorro, and explore the cave dwellings of the Mogollon people.

Las Cruces

★ **New Mexico Farm and Ranch Heritage Museum:** New Mexico State University hosts this museum that honors the state's farming and ranching history. The museum is also a working farm, where you can meet churro sheep and watch cows getting milked.

Socorro

★ **Very Large Array:** Satellite dishes that bring TV shows into homes are specks compared to the 27 dishes at the Very Large Array. Each one is 82 feet (25 m) wide and weighs 235 tons! Stop by and learn more about how picking up radio waves from space helps scientists learn about the universe.

Mineral Hot Springs

Truth or Consequences

★ **Mineral Hot Springs:** Long before the Anglos came to New Mexico, Native Americans soothed aches and pains in the waters of the hot springs here. The mineral-filled water bubbles up from under the ground.

Silver City

★ **Gila Cliff Dwellings National Monument:** Not much has changed in the cliffs since the Mogollon people lived there more than 700 years ago. Visitors can explore several dozen rooms that were once part of a Mogollon village.

FAQ

Q: HOW DID TRUTH OR CONSEQUENCES, NEW MEXICO, GET ITS NAME?

A: In 1950, *Truth or Consequences* was the name of a popular radio show (later it was also on television). The show's producers said it would broadcast live from any town that changed its name to Truth or Consequences. The residents of Hot Springs went along with the offer. Today, the town is also sometimes called T or C.

Visitors at Gila Cliff Dwellings National Monument

SOUTH-EASTERN NEW MEXICO

THINGS TO DO: Learn about UFOs (unidentified flying objects), slide down white sand dunes, and see hundreds of thousands of bats.

Alamogordo

★ **New Mexico Museum of Space History:** Scientists in New Mexico have played a big part in space exploration. Learn more about their achievements at the state's museum of space history. The museum is also home to the International Space Hall of Fame.

★ **White Sands National Monument:** It's been said that White Sands is like no other place on Earth. Many visitors are stunned by this huge stretch of whiteness, which constantly shifts with the wind. Hiking, bird-watching, and biking are popular activities at the monument.

White Sands National Monument

SEE IT HERE!

ALIENS AMONG US?

Want to find out more about UFOs? Then Roswell is the place to go—it's the home of the International UFO Museum! In 1947, residents around Roswell thought they saw a "flying saucer," or UFO. At first, the U.S. government reported it was a UFO, but then officials said it was just a weather balloon. Whatever it was, Roswell became a center for people who believe that UFOs and space aliens are real.

International UFO Museum

Fort Sumner

★ **Old Fort Sumner Museum:** Wild West outlaw Billy the Kid is buried at Old Fort Sumner. Just a short walk from the museum is a monument that honors the memory of 19th-century Apaches and Navajos, who were forced to live at the fort before being moved to reservations.

SEE IT HERE!

WESTERN HERITAGE MUSEUM

Hobbs, near the Texas border, is the home of the Western Heritage Museum. The museum opened a new building in 2006. It's filled with information about the cowboys and ranchers who once lived in New Mexico and across the Southwest. The museum also houses the Lea County Cowboy Hall of Fame. The region around Hobbs claims more world-champion rodeo cowboys than any other part of the world.

Carlsbad

★ **Living Desert Zoo and Gardens State Park:** Mountain lions, rattlesnakes, and bears, oh my! These desert dwellers and more can be seen at this park, where injured wild animals are taken to heal before going back into the wild.

The park also has many kinds of cacti and other desert plants.

★ **Carlsbad Caverns National Park:** Watch bats soar off for their evening meals, or get your hands dirty on a cave tour. These are just two of the fun events waiting at Carlsbad Caverns. In the underground caves, the temperature is always a cool 56°F (13°C).

A cave at Carlsbad Caverns called the **Big Room** is about the size of eight football fields!

The Big Room at Carlsbad Caverns

WRITING PROJECTS

Check out these ideas for creating campaign brochures and writing you-are-there editorials. Or research famous New Mexicans.

118

ART PROJECTS

Create a great PowerPoint presentation, illustrate the state song, or research the state quarter and design your own.

119

NEW MEXICO
1912
LAND OF ENCHANTMENT
2008
E PLURIBUS UNUM

TIMELINE

What happened when? This timeline highlights important events in the state's history—and shows what was happening throughout the United States at the same time.

122

FAST FACTS

Use this section to find fascinating facts about state symbols, land area and population statistics, weather, sports teams, and much more.

126

GLOSSARY

Remember the Words to Know from the chapters in this book? They're all collected here.

125

SCIENCE, TECHNOLOGY, & MATH PROJECTS

Make weather maps, graph population statistics, and research endangered species that live in the state.

120

PRIMARY VS. SECONDARY SOURCES

121

So what are primary and secondary sources? And what's the diff? This section explains all that and where you can find them.

BIOGRAPHICAL DICTIONARY

133

This at-a-glance guide highlights some of the state's most important and influential people. Visit this section and read about their contributions to the state, the country, and the world.

RESOURCES

Books, Web sites, DVDs, and more. Take a look at these additional sources for information about the state.

137

WRITING PROJECTS

★ ★ ★

Write a Memoir, Journal, or Editorial for Your School Newspaper!

Picture Yourself . . .

★ As a Native American, African American, or woman in early New Mexico, struggling to attain the full rights of citizenship, including the right to vote.

★ In your research, read about Miguel Trujillo and Adelina Otero-Warren.

★ Explain what reasons the government gave for denying certain groups their basic rights as citizens. What actions do you take to win the right to vote?

SEE: Chapter Four, pages 46–47, and Chapter Five, pages 56–57, 62.

GO TO: www.kvtb.org/pdf/6-8_TheRightToVote_Sept.pdf; www.constitutioncenter.org/explore/ForKids/index.shtml

Create an Election Brochure or Web Site!

Run for office! Throughout this book, you've read about some of the issues that concern New Mexico today. As a candidate for governor of New Mexico, create a campaign brochure or Web site.

★ Explain how you meet the qualifications to be governor of New Mexico.

★ Talk about the three or four major issues you'll focus on if you're elected.

★ Remember, you'll be responsible for New Mexico's budget. How would you spend the taxpayers' money?

SEE: Chapter Seven, pages 85–86.

GO TO: The New Mexico government Web site at www.newmexico.gov

Create an interview script with a famous person from New Mexico!

★ Research various famous New Mexicans, such as Brian Urlacher, Nancy Lopez, Maria Martinez, Billy the Kid, and many others.

★ Based on your research, pick one person you would most like to interview.

★ Write a script of the interview. What questions would you ask? How would this famous person answer? Create a question-and-answer format. You may want to supplement this writing project with a voice-recording dramatization of the interview.

SEE: Chapter Six, pages 74–79, and the Biographical Dictionary, page 133–136.

Nancy Lopez

ART PROJECTS

★ ★ ★

Illustrate the Lyrics to the New Mexico State Songs
("O Fair New Mexico" and "Así Es Nuevo Méjico")

Use markers, paints, photos, collages, colored pencils, or computer graphics to illustrate the lyrics to "O Fair New Mexico" and "Así Es Nuevo Méjico." Turn your illustrations into a picture book, or scan them into PowerPoint and add music.

SEE: The lyrics to both state songs on page 128.

Create a PowerPoint Presentation or Visitors' Guide
Welcome to New Mexico!

New Mexico is a great place to visit and to live! From its natural beauty to its bustling cities and historical sites, there's plenty to see and do. In your PowerPoint presentation or brochure, highlight 10 to 15 of New Mexico's fascinating landmarks. Be sure to include:

★ a map of the state showing where these sites are located

★ photos, illustrations, Web links, natural history facts, geographic stats, climate and weather, plants and wildlife, and recent discoveries

SEE: Chapter One, pages 9–21, and Chapter Nine, pages 103–115.

GO TO: The official Web site of the New Mexico Tourism Department at www.newmexico.org. Download and print maps, photos, national landmark images, and vacation ideas for tourists.

State Quarter Project

From 1999 to 2008, the U.S. Mint introduced new quarters commemorating each of the 50 states in the order that they were admitted to the Union. Each state's quarter features a unique design on its back, or reverse.

★ Research the significance of the image. Who designed the quarter? Who chose the final design?

★ Design your own New Mexico state quarter. What images would you choose for the reverse?

★ Make a poster showing the New Mexico quarter and label each image.

SCIENCE, TECHNOLOGY, & MATH PROJECTS

★ ★ ★

Graph Population Statistics!

★ Compare population statistics (such as ethnic background, birth, death, and literacy rates) in New Mexico counties or major cities.

★ In your graph or chart, look at population density and write sentences describing what the population statistics show; graph one set of population statistics and write a paragraph explaining what the graphs reveal.

SEE: Chapter Six, pages 65–70.

GO TO: The official Web site for the U.S. Census Bureau at www.census.gov, and at http://quickfacts.census.gov/qfd/states/35000.html, to find out more about population statistics, how they work, and what the statistics are for New Mexico.

Create a Weather Map of New Mexico!

Use your knowledge of New Mexico's geography to research and identify conditions that result in specific weather events. What is it about the geography of New Mexico that makes it vulnerable to droughts? Create a weather map or poster that shows the weather patterns over the state, or display wet and dry years between 1895 and the present. Include a caption explaining the technology used to measure weather phenomena such as droughts and provide data.

SEE: Chapter One, pages 17–18.

GO TO: The National Oceanic and Atmospheric Administration's National Weather Service Web site at www.weather.gov for weather maps and forecasts for New Mexico.

Mexican spotted owl

Track Endangered Species

Using your knowledge of New Mexico's wildlife, research which animals and plants are endangered or threatened.

★ Find out what the state is doing to protect these species.

★ Chart known populations of the animals and plants, and report on changes in certain geographic areas.

SEE: Chapter One, page 21.

GO TO: The U.S. Fish and Wildlife site at http://ecos.fws.gov/tess_public/StateListing.do?state=NM&status=listed

PRIMARY VS. SECONDARY SOURCES

★　★　★

What's the Diff?

Your teacher may require at least one or two primary sources and one or two secondary sources for your assignment. So, what's the difference between the two?

★ **Primary sources are original.** You are reading the actual words of someone's diary, journal, letter, autobiography, or interview. Primary sources can also be photographs, maps, prints, cartoons, news/film footage, posters, first-person newspaper articles, drawings, musical scores, and recordings. By the way, when you conduct a survey, interview someone, shoot a video, or take photographs to include in a project, you are creating primary sources!

★ **Secondary sources are what you find in encyclopedias, textbooks, articles, biographies, and almanacs.** These are written by a person or group of people who tell about something that happened to someone else. Secondary sources also recount what another person said or did. This book is an example of a secondary source.

Now that you know what primary sources are—where can you find them?

★ **Your school or local library:** Check the library catalog for collections of original writings, government documents, musical scores, and so on. Some of this material may be stored on microfilm. The Library of Congress Web site (www.loc.gov) is an excellent online resource for primary source materials.

★ **Historical societies:** These organizations keep historical documents, photographs, and other materials. Staff members can help you find what you are looking for. History museums are also great places to see primary sources firsthand.

★ **The Internet:** There are lots of sites that have primary sources you can download and use in a project or assignment.

TIMELINE

★ ★ ★

U.S. Events	BCE	New Mexico Events

Chaco Pueblo

c. 9000 BCE
Hunters track animals near what is now Clovis.

1 CE

c. 850 CE
The Anasazis begin to build towns in Chaco Canyon.

1400

1492
Christopher Columbus and his crew sight land in the Caribbean Sea.

1500

1539
Marcos de Niza and Estevanico lead the first Spanish expedition into New Mexico.

1565
Spanish admiral Pedro Menéndez de Avilés founds St. Augustine, Florida, the oldest continuously occupied European settlement in the continental United States.

1598
Juan de Oñate leads Spanish settlers to the Rio Grande valley.

1600

1607
The first permanent English settlement in North America is established at Jamestown.

1610
Santa Fe becomes the capital of New Mexico.

1620
Pilgrims found Plymouth Colony, the second permanent English settlement.

1680
Pueblo people rebel and drive the Spanish from New Mexico.

1682
René-Robert Cavelier, Sieur de La Salle, claims more than 1 million square miles (2.6 million sq km) of territory in the Mississippi River basin for France, naming it Louisiana.

1692
Spain regains control of New Mexico.

1700

1706
Albuquerque is founded.

1776
Thirteen American colonies declare their independence from Great Britain.

U.S. Events

New Mexico Events

1787
The U.S. Constitution is written.

`1800`

1803
The Louisiana Purchase almost doubles the size of the United States.

1821
New Mexico becomes part of the independent nation of Mexico; William Becknell opens the Santa Fe Trail.

1830
The Indian Removal Act forces eastern Native American groups to relocate west of the Mississippi River.

1846-48
The United States fights a war with Mexico over western territories in the Mexican War.

1846
U.S. forces invade New Mexico and eventually take it from Spain.

1850
New Mexico becomes a U.S. territory.

1853
The Gadsden Purchase adds some Mexican lands to New Mexico.

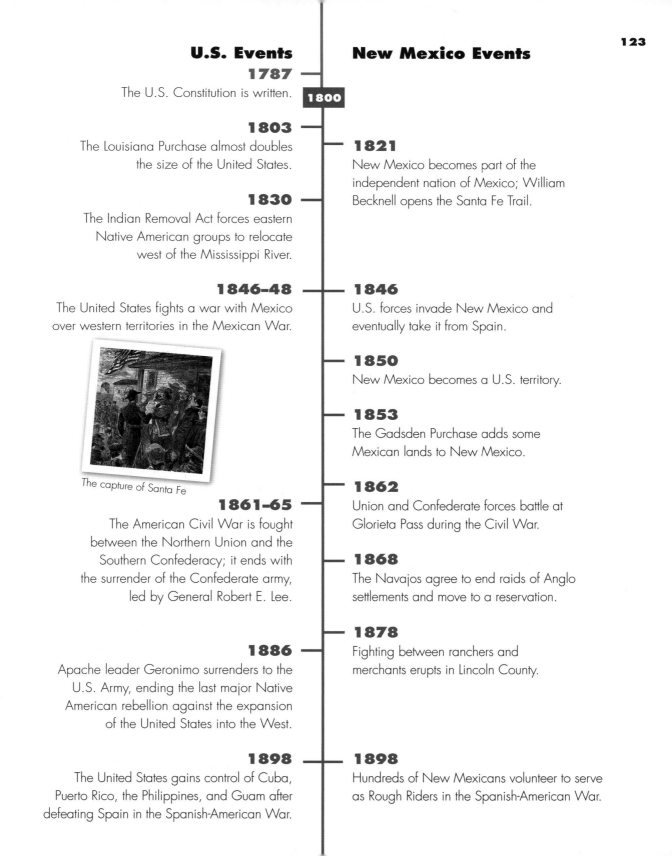
The capture of Santa Fe

1862
Union and Confederate forces battle at Glorieta Pass during the Civil War.

1861-65
The American Civil War is fought between the Northern Union and the Southern Confederacy; it ends with the surrender of the Confederate army, led by General Robert E. Lee.

1868
The Navajos agree to end raids of Anglo settlements and move to a reservation.

1878
Fighting between ranchers and merchants erupts in Lincoln County.

1886
Apache leader Geronimo surrenders to the U.S. Army, ending the last major Native American rebellion against the expansion of the United States into the West.

1898
The United States gains control of Cuba, Puerto Rico, the Philippines, and Guam after defeating Spain in the Spanish-American War.

1898
Hundreds of New Mexicans volunteer to serve as Rough Riders in the Spanish-American War.

U.S. Events **1900** New Mexico Events

1908
George McJunkin finds bones
of the Folsom people.

1917–18
The United States engages in World War I.

1912
New Mexico becomes the 47th state.

1916
Mexican rebel Pancho Villa raids
Columbus, New Mexico.

1929
The stock market crashes, plunging the United
States more deeply into the Great Depression.

1930s
New Deal programs provide jobs
for New Mexicans; archaeologists
find bones of the Clovis people.

1941–45
The United States engages in World War II.

1945
The world's first atomic bomb is tested
at the Trinity site near Alamogordo.

1948
Miguel Trujillo helps Native Americans
in New Mexico win the right to vote.

1951–53
The United States engages
in the Korean War.

1964–73
The United States engages
in the Vietnam War.

2000

2001
Terrorists hijack four U.S. aircraft and crash
them into the World Trade Center in New
York City, the Pentagon in Arlington, Virginia,
and a Pennsylvania field, killing thousands.

2002
Bill Richardson is elected
governor of New Mexico.

Governor Bill Richardson

2003
The United States and coalition
forces invade Iraq.

2006
Plans begin for building a fence between
New Mexico and Mexico in an attempt
to prevent undocumented immigrants
from entering New Mexico.

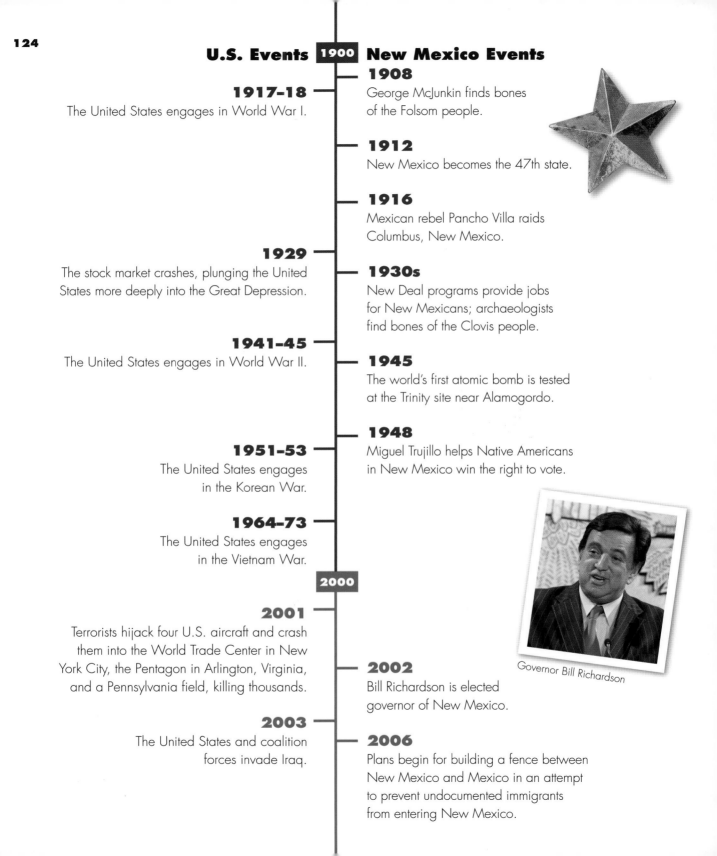

GLOSSARY

★ ★ ★

abolished put an end to

ancestral relating to an ancestor, or a family member from the distant past

archaeologists people who study the remains of past human societies

artifacts items created by humans, usually for a practical purpose

aviation the design and manufacture of airplanes

cavalry soldiers who ride on horseback

constitution a written document that contains all the governing principles of a state or country

endangered in danger of becoming extinct

erosion the gradual wearing away of rock or soil by physical breakdown, chemical solution, or water

fossils the remains or prints of ancient animals or plants left in stone

gorge a narrow, steep-walled canyon

missionaries people who try to convert others to a religion

petition a list of voters' signatures requesting some action

petrified changed into a stony hardness

plateau an elevated part of the earth with steep slopes

prejudiced having an unreasonable hatred or fear of others

reservoirs artificial lakes or tanks created for water storage

rituals religious ceremonies or social customs

semiarid receiving 10 to 20 inches (25 to 50 cm) of rain every year

suffrage the right to vote

tram a carrier that travels on overhead rails or cables

undocumented lacking documents required for legal immigration or residence

FAST FACTS

★ ★ ★

State Symbols

State seal

Statehood date	January 6, 1912, the 47th state
Origin of state name	From the Spanish name La Nueva Mexico, which in English is "New Mexico"
State capital	Santa Fe
State nickname	The Land of Enchantment
State motto	*Crescit Eundo* ("It grows as it goes")
State bird	Roadrunner
State flower	Yucca
State animal	Black bear
State fish	Cutthroat trout
State fossil	*Coelophysis*
State gem	Turquoise
State insect	Tarantula Hawk Wasp
State songs	"*Así Es Nuevo Méjico*" and "O Fair New Mexico"
State grass	Blue grama
State tree	Piñon, or nut pine
State fair	Albuquerque (mid-September)

Geography

Total area; rank	121,590 square miles (314,918 sq km); 5th
Land; rank	121,356 square miles (314,310 sq km); 5th
Water; rank	234 square miles (606 sq km); 49th
Inland water; rank	234 square miles (606 sq km); 45th
Geographic center	Torrance County, 12 miles (19 km) southwest of Willard
Latitude	31°20′ N to 37° N
Longitude	103° W to 109° W
Highest point	Wheeler Peak, 13,161 feet (4,011 m), located in Taos
Lowest point	Red Bluff Reservoir, 2,842 feet (866 m), located in Eddy
Largest city	Albuquerque
Number of counties	33
Longest river	Rio Grande

Population

Population; rank (2006 estimate)	1,954,599; 36th
Density (2006 estimate)	16 persons per square mile (6 per sq km)
Population distribution (2000 census)	75% urban, 25% rural
Race (2005 estimate)	White persons: 84.5%*
	American Indian and Alaska Native persons: 10.2%*
	Black persons: 2.4%*
	Asian persons: 1.3%*
	Native Hawaiian and Other Pacific Islander: 0.1%*
	Persons reporting two or more races: 1.5%
	Persons of Hispanic or Latino origin: 43.4%[†]
	White persons not Hispanic: 43.1%

Includes persons reporting only one race.

[†] *Hispanics may be of any race, so they are also included in applicable race categories.*

Weather

Record high temperature	122°F (50°C) at Waste Isolation Pilot Plant, near Carlsbad, on June 27, 1994
Record low temperature	−50°F (−46°C) at Gavilan, near Lindrith, on February 1, 1951
Average July temperature	79°F (26°C)
Average January temperature	36°F (2°C)
Average annual precipitation	9 inches (23 cm)

State flag

STATE SONGS

New Mexico has two state songs, one in English and one in Spanish. "O Fair New Mexico," words and music by Elizabeth Garrett, was adopted in 1917. "Así Es Nuevo Méjico," words and music by Amadeo Lucero, was adopted in 1971.

"O Fair New Mexico"

Under a sky of azure, where balmy breezes blow,
Kissed by the golden sunshine, is Nuevo Méjico.
Home of the Montezuma, with fiery heart aglow,
State of the deeds historic, is Nuevo Méjico.

Chorus:
O fair New Mexico, we love, we love you so,
Our hearts with pride o'erflow, no matter where
   we go,
O fair New Mexico, we love you, we love you so,
The grandest state to know, New Mexico.

(Chorus)
Rugged and high sierras, with deep canyons below,
Dotted with fertile valleys, is Nuevo Méjico.
Fields full of sweet alfalfa, richest perfumes bestow,
State of apple blossoms, is Nuevo Méjico.

(Chorus)
Days that are full of heart-dreams, nights when the
   moon hangs low,
Beaming its benediction, o'er Nuevo Méjico.
Land with its bright mañana [tomorrow], coming
   through weal and woe,
State of our esperanza [hope] is Nuevo Méjico.

"Así Es Nuevo Méjico"

Un canto que traigo muy dentro del alma
Lo canto a mi estado, mi tierra natal.
De flores dorada mi tierra encantada
De lindas mujeres, que no tiene igual.

Chorus:
Así es Nuevo Méjico
Así es esta tierra del sol
De sierras y valles, de tierras frutales
Así es Nuevo Méjico.
El negro, el hispano, el anglo, y el indio,
todos son tus hijos, todos por igual.
Tus pueblos, y aldeas, mi tierra encantada
De lindas mujeres que no tiene igual.

(Chorus)
El Río del Norte que es el Río Grande
Sus aguas corrientes fluyen hasta el mar,
Y riegan tus campos
Mi tierra encantada de lindas mujeres
Que no tiene igual.

(Chorus)
Tus campos se visten de flores de mayo,
De lindos colores que Diós les dotó
Tus pájaros cantan, mi tierra encantada,
Sus trinos de amores al ser celestial.

(Chorus)
Mi tierra encantada de historia bañada
Tan linda, tan bella, sin comparación.
Te rindo homenaje, te rindo cariño
Soldado valiente, te rinde su amor.

For the English translation, see http://en.wikipedia.org/wiki/Asi_Es_Nuevo_México

NATURAL AREAS AND HISTORIC SITES

★ ★ ★

National Park
Carlsbad Caverns National Park, the state's only national park, features a series of connected caverns and has one of the world's largest underground spaces.

National Monuments
New Mexico features 10 national monuments, including *Aztec Ruins National Monument; Bandelier National Monument; Capulin Volcano National Monument; El Malpais National Monument; El Morro National Monument; Fort Union National Monument; Gila Cliff Dwellings National Monument; Petroglyph National Monument; Salinas Pueblo Missions National Monument; White Sands National Monument.*

National Historical Parks
Chaco Culture National Historical Park, the site of a major urban center of ancestral Puebloan cultures, preserves some of the finest ancient structures in the United States.

The *Pecos National Historical Park* preserves 12,000 years of history, including the ancient pueblo of Pecos, two Spanish colonial missions, Santa Fe Trail sites, the site of the Civil War Battle of Glorieta Pass, and 20th-century ranch history.

National Historic Trails
El Camino Real de Tierra Adentro National Historic Trail is a trail that features more than 300 years of heritage and culture in the Southwest.

The *Old Spanish National Historic Trail* passes through six different states, linking Santa Fe to Los Angeles, California.

The *Santa Fe National Historic Trail* is another trail that passes through five states, linking Missouri to New Mexico.

State Parks and Forests
The New Mexico state park system maintains 33 state parks and recreation areas, including *Cimarron Canyon State Park, Oasis State Park, Rio Grande Nature Center State Park*, and *Ute Lake State Park.*

SPORTS TEAMS

★ ★ ★

NCAA Teams (Division I)

University of New Mexico *Lobos*
New Mexico State University *Aggies*

New Mexico State basketball players celebrating a win

CULTURAL INSTITUTIONS

★ ★ ★

Libraries

Albuquerque Public Library is the largest public library in the state.

The *New Mexico State Library* has been a leader in the development of New Mexico's public libraries, helping them to build the programs needed by their communities. The library features a Southwest special collections department.

Museums

The *Albuquerque Museum* (Albuquerque) has a fine collection of European and Native American art.

Bradbury Science Museum (Los Alamos) shows the development of atomic energy.

El Rancho de las Golondrinas (Santa Fe) re-creates life among the Hispanic settlers of New Mexico in the early 1700s.

Museum of New Mexico (Santa Fe) located in the Palace of the Governors includes the Museum of Fine Arts, the Museum of Indian Arts, and the Museum of International Folk Art.

The Wheelwright Museum of the American Indian (Santa Fe) hosts changing exhibitions of contemporary and historic Native American art with an emphasis on the Southwest.

Performing Arts

New Mexico has two major opera companies, one major symphony orchestra, and one major dance company.

Universities and Colleges

In 2006, New Mexico had 26 public and 12 private institutions of higher learning.

ANNUAL EVENTS

January–March

King's Day Dances in most of the pueblos (January 6)

Winter Festival in Red River (January)

Winter Ski Fiesta in Santa Fe (February)

Rio Grande Arts and Crafts Festival in Albuquerque (early March)

April–June

Green Corn Dance at San Felipe Pueblo (May 1)

Four Corners Hot Air Balloon Fiesta near Farmington (late May)

Taos Spring Arts Celebration (May–June)

Sandia Classic Hang Gliding Competition in Albuquerque (June)

New Mexico Arts and Crafts Fair in Albuquerque (late June)

July–September

Apache Indian Ceremonial in Mescalero (Fourth of July weekend)

Rodeo de Santa Fe (mid-July)

"Billy the Kid" Pageant in Lincoln (early August)

Inter-Tribal Indian Ceremonial in Gallup (mid-August)

Santa Fe Indian Market (late August)

Great American Duck Race in Deming (late August)

Hatch Chile Festival in Hatch (September)

All-American Futurity Horse Race in Ruidoso (September)

Whole Enchilada Fiesta in Las Cruces (September)

Fiesta de Santa Fe (mid-September)

New Mexico State Fair in Albuquerque (mid-September)

Feast Day in Taos Pueblo (late September)

October–December

Festival of the Arts in Santa Fe (early October)

Navajo Fair in Shiprock (early October)

Taos Festival of Arts (early October)

International Balloon Fiesta in Albuquerque (mid-October)

Winter Spanish Market in Santa Fe (December)

Red Rock Balloon Rally in Gallup (December)

Farolito Walk on Canyon Road in Santa Fe (December 24)

Christmas Eve Dances in mission churches at many pueblos (December 24)

BIOGRAPHICAL DICTIONARY

Rudolfo Anaya (1937–), a writer born in Pastura, is best known for his book *Bless Me, Ultima*. He taught for many years at the University of New Mexico.

Elfego Baca (1865–1945) was a sheriff in Socorro County who became famous for a shoot-out with Texas outlaws. He later became a lawyer and politician.

Jimmy Santiago Baca (1952–) is a writer from Santa Fe with a mixed Hispanic and Native American family background. He has won awards for his poetry and a book about his life.

William "Billy the Kid" Bonney See page 50.

Kit Carson See page 49.

Francisco Vásquez de Coronado (c. 1510–1544) was a Spanish explorer who led an expedition into New Mexico and the surrounding area in 1540.

Geronimo

R. C. Gorman

Estevanico (?–1539) was a former enslaved African who traveled with Marcos de Niza to New Mexico in 1539. Estevanico was the first outsider to encounter the Pueblo people. He was killed at Zuni Pueblo.

Joe Garcia See page 89.

Geronimo (1829–1909) was a leader of the Chiricahua Apaches who was born in what is now western New Mexico. In the 1880s, he fought U.S. troops while trying to avoid being forced onto a reservation.

Robert Goddard See page 58.

R. C. Gorman (1931–2005) was a prominent Navajo artist, renowned for his colorful images of Native American women. Born in Arizona, he moved to Taos in 1968. There he opened the Navajo Gallery, the first art gallery owned by a Native American.

Sid Gutierrez (1951–), an astronaut born in Albuquerque, was the first Latino to lead a space shuttle mission.

William Hanna (1910–2001) teamed up with Joseph Barbera to create cartoon characters such as Tom and Jerry and Scooby-Doo. Over his long career, Hanna won seven Academy Awards and eight Emmy Awards. He was born in Melrose.

Tony Hillerman (1925–) writes popular mystery novels set on Navajo lands in New Mexico. He lives in Albuquerque.

Conrad Hilton See page 101.

Allan Houser (1915–1994) was a Chiricahua Apache sculptor who studied and worked in Santa Fe. He is known for his graceful statues of Native Americans.

Jean Baptiste Lamy (1814–1888) was a Roman Catholic priest who built many churches and schools in New Mexico.

Tony Hillerman

Octaviano Larrazolo See page 86.

George López See page 75.

Nancy Lopez See page 79.

Mabel Dodge Luhan (1879–1962) was a wealthy world traveler who settled in Taos. She invited painter Georgia O'Keeffe, photographer Ansel Adams, and other artists and writers to stay at her home, helping make Taos a center for the arts.

Antonio José Martínez (1795–1867) was a Native American priest who championed the rights of the Pueblo. He set up the first school in Taos and had the first printing press in New Mexico.

Esther Martinez (1912–2006) was a storyteller who drew on her Native American culture. She was a native of the Ohkay Owingeh (San Juan) Pueblo.

Maria Martinez See page 74.

George McJunkin See page 25.

N. Scott Momaday See page 70.

Roy Nakayama See page 96.

Maria Martinez

Marcos de Niza (c. 1495–1558) was an Italian priest who, in 1539, led the first European expedition into New Mexico. He claimed to have found one of the Seven Cities of Cíbola during the trip, prompting further exploration of the region.

Georgia O'Keeffe See page 76.

Juan de Oñate (c. 1550–1626) was a wealthy merchant in New Spain who led the first band of European settlers into New Mexico. As governor of New Mexico, he treated the Pueblo people brutally and was later tried for his cruel actions.

J. Robert Oppenheimer (1904–1967) was a scientist who ran the Manhattan Project at Los Alamos. He and his team of 3,000 people developed the first atomic bomb.

Katherine Ortega (1934–) served as the U.S. treasurer from 1983 to 1989. She is a native of Tularosa.

Katherine Ortega

Alfonso Ortiz See page 30.

Adelina Otero-Warren See page 57.

Popé (?–1692) was a San Juan Pueblo priest who wanted to preserve Pueblo life. He and other priests urged the Pueblo to resist Spanish culture and religion. In 1680, they led the Pueblo Revolt, which drove the Spaniards from the region.

Ernie Pyle (1900–1945) was a journalist who lived for a time in Albuquerque. He wrote about U.S. soldiers during World War II and was killed during combat in the Pacific.

Bill Richardson See page 85.

Millie Santillanes See page 108.

Luci Tapahonso (1953–) is a Navajo poet from Shiprock. She was raised in a household where little English was spoken. To this day, she writes her poetry in the Navajo language and then translates it into English.

Luci Tapahonso

Miguel Trujillo See page 62.

Al Unser (1939–) is part of an Albuquerque family famous for producing top race-car drivers. He is one of only three people to win the Indianapolis 500 four times. His son **Al Unser Jr. (1962–)** has won the Indianapolis 500 twice.

Brian Urlacher (1978–) is one of the top linebackers in the National Football League. Born in Washington State, he moved to Lovington, New Mexico, as a child and later became a top college player at the University of New Mexico.

Don Diego de Vargas (?–1704) was a Spanish soldier who led the reconquest of New Mexico in 1692, after the Pueblos had driven Spanish settlers from the colony.

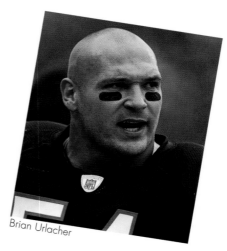
Brian Urlacher

Susan Wallace See page 52.

Annie Dodge Wauneka See page 63.

Jim White See page 16.

Cathay Williams (1842–1924) was born into slavery in Missouri. During the Civil War, she disguised herself as a man and served as a soldier. She later was sent to New Mexico and was part of the Buffalo Soldiers.

Cheryl Willman See page 100.

Heather Wilson (1960–) is a congresswoman from New Mexico. She was also one of the first women to graduate from the U.S. Air Force Academy.

Al Unser Jr.

RESOURCES

BOOKS

Nonfiction

Anderson, Dale. *The Atom Bomb Project*. Milwaukee, Wis.: World Almanac Library, 2004.

Blue, Rose, and Corinne J. Naden. *Exploring the Southwestern United States*. Chicago: Raintree, 2004.

Iverson, Peter, ed. *For Our Navajo People: Diné Letters, Speeches, and Petitions, 1900–1960*. Albuquerque: University of New Mexico Press, 2002.

Mattern, Joanne. *Georgia O'Keeffe*. Edina, Minn.: Abdo Publishing, 2005.

Miller, Raymond. *The Apache*. Farmington Hills, Mich.: KidHaven Press, 2005.

St. Lawrence, Genevieve. *The Pueblo and Their History*. Minneapolis: Compass Point Books, 2006.

Stefoff, Rebecca. *American Voices from the Wild West*. New York: Marshall Cavendish Benchmark, 2007.

Vivian, R. Gwinn, and Margaret J. Anderson. *Chaco Canyon*. New York: Oxford University Press, 2002.

Fiction

Abraham, Susan Gonzales. *Cecilia's Year*. El Paso, Tex.: Cinco Puntos Press, 2004.

Anaya, Rudolfo. *Bless Me, Ultima*. New York: Warner Books, 1994.

Anaya, Rudolfo. *Serafina's Stories*. Albuquerque: University of New Mexico Press, 2004.

Little, Kimberley Griffiths. *The Last Snake Runner*. New York: Dell Laurel-Leaf, 2004.

Taschek, Karen. *Horse of Seven Moons*. Albuquerque: University of New Mexico Press, 2004.

DVDs

Buffalo Soldiers. Burbank, Calif.: Warner Home Video, 2006.
The Mystery of Chaco Canyon. Oley, Pa.: Bullfrog Films, 1999.
Six Days in Roswell. Novi, Mich.: Synapse Films, 1999.
The West. Los Angeles: PBS Home Video/Paramount Home Entertainment, 2004.

WEB SITES AND ORGANIZATIONS

Carlsbad Caverns National Park
www.nps.gov/cave/
Visit this site for more information about the caves and visiting them.

Museum of Spanish Colonial Art
www.spanishcolonial.org/
See examples of Spanish colonial art from New Mexico.

The Navajo Nation
www.navajo.org/
The official Navajo Web site has information about Navajo history and the tribe today.

New Mexico Tourism Department
www.newmexico.org
An overview of the most popular tourist sites in New Mexico.

Pueblos of New Mexico
www.newmexico.org/directory/page/DB-directory-pueblos.html
For links to the Web sites of the 19 pueblos of New Mexico.

Sipapu–The Anasazi Emergence into the Cyber World
http://sipapu.gsu.edu
Visit this site to explore the history of the Anasazis.

Soul of New Mexico
www.soulofnewmexico.com
Visit this site to learn more about the history of New Mexico's African American residents.

The State of New Mexico
www.newmexico.gov
The official state Web site provides lots of information plus links to other state sites.

INDEX

★ ★ ★

Abiquiu, *8*
Abruzzo, Ben, *79*
Acoma people, 36, 38, 105, *105*
Adams, Ansel, 134
adobe, *27*, *40*, *42*, *43*, *54*, 68
African Americans, 47, 50, 51, 52, 65, 70
agriculture, 25, 30, 93, 94, 96, 97, *97*
Alamogordo, 60, *60*, 96, 114
Albuquerque, 11, *22*, 40, 49, 61, 66, 71, *71*, 78, *87*, 107–108
Anasazi people, 25, 27–28, *27*, *29*, 36, 77, 96, 104
Anaya, Rudolfo, 77–78, *77*, 133
Anderson, Maxie, 79
Anglos, 44–45, 52, 65, 69–70
animal life, 11, 14, 15, 20–21, *20*, 24, 25, 50, 69, 93, 94, *94*, 106, 115
Apache people, 30–31, 49, 51, *51*, 69, 76
Armijo, Manuel, 45
arroyos (dry riverbeds), 18
art, 61, 74, 76–77, *76*, 107, *107*, 133
atomic bombs, 60, *60*
auto racing, 79, 136, *136*
aviation industry, 99, 100
Aztec, 104
Aztec Ruins National Monument, 104

Baca, Elfego, 133
Baca, Ezequiel Cabeza de, *57*
Baca, Jimmy Santiago, 133
"badlands," 17
Bahe, Henry, Jr., *59*
bald eagles, 21
ballooning, 79
Bandelier National Monument, 58, *101*, 111
Bandera Center, 105
Basin and Range region, 13, 15–16

basins, 15
Battle of Glorieta Pass, 49
Battle of Valverde, 49
Becknell, William, 44
Bee, Tom, *77*
Bent, Charles, 45
Billy the Kid. *See* Bonney, William.
birds, 20, 21, *21*
bison, 14
blue grama (state grass), 14
Blue Hole, 106, *106*
Blumenschein, Ernest, 76, *76*
Bonney, William, 50, *50*
boom towns, 50
borders, 10, 15, 46, 62–63
Box Trail, *8*
Bradbury Science Museum, 111, *111*
Bremer, Jose, *84*
Buffalo Soldiers, 48, 51, 70, 136

cacti, 18, *18*, 115
Canadian River, 14
Capulin Volcano National Monument, 12, 106
Carlsbad, 85, 115
Carlsbad Caverns National Park, 15, 16, 115, *115*
Carson, Christopher "Kit," 49, *49*, 51, 109
Castilla, Don Pedro Lorenzo de, 36
Cather, Willa, 47
cattle, 36, 50, 93, 94, *94*
caves, 15, 16, 24, 29, 115
Chaco Canyon, 27, 28, 29, 104
Chaco Culture National Historical Park, 28, 104
Chama, 109
Chavez, Dennis, *57*
Chihuahuan Desert, 15
chile peppers, 72, *72*, 73, 96
Chisum, John, 50
Cíbola (Seven Cities of Gold), 34, 35, 104, 135
Cimarron, 50, 106

City of Las Vegas Museum, 106
Civilian Conservation Corps (CCC), 58
Civil War, 47–49, 136
climate, 17–18, 25, 99
Clinton, Bill, 85
Clovis people, 24
"code talkers," 59, *59*
Coelophysis (dinosaur), 11
Colorado Plateau, 13, 17
Columbus, 56
Comanche people, 51
commissioners of public lands, 86
communications, 67
Confederate States of America, 48
Coronado, Francisco Vásquez de, 35, 133
counties, *88*, 89
court of appeals, 87
cowboys, 50, 72, 73, 94, 115
crafts, 25, 29, *29*, 74–75, *74*, *105*
Cumbres and Toltec Scenic Railroad, 109

dance, 30, 39, 77, 78, *78*
Deming, 62, 85
Diamond Ranch, *94*
dinosaurs, 11–12, 17, 107
district courts, 87
Domenici, Pete, 81

Eagle Ranch, 96
Eclipse Aviation, 100
education, 47, 63, 66, 71, *71*, 84–85, 86
elections, 57, 62, 85, 89
electricity, 68, 98, 105
elevation, 9, *10*, 11, 15, 19
Elizabethtown, 50
El Malpais National Monument, 17, 105, *105*
El Morro National Monument, 36, 105
El Rancho de las Golondrinas, 111
endangered species, 21, *21*

environmental protection, 21
Estevanico (explorer) *32*, 33, 34, 35, 133
ethnic groups, 69–70
European exploration, *7*, *32*, 33, *37*, 133, 135
European settlers, 35–36, 38, 39–40, *39*, 41, 43, 52, 69, *75*, 135
executive branch of government, 82, 83, 85–86
The Extraordinary Affray (Ernest Blumenschein), *76*

farolitos (Christmas decorations), 40, *78*
folklorico (folk dancing), *77*
Folsom people, 24, *24*
foods, 24, 25, 29, 30, *31*, 36, *72*, *72*, *73*, *73*
Fort Craig, 49
Fort Sumner, 50, 115
Fort Union, *47*, *48*, 49
fossils, 11–12, 17
Four Corners region, 25, 51
French settlers, 41

Gadsden Purchase, 46
Gallup, 66, 71
Garcia, Joe, 89, *89*
Gavilan, 17
Georgia O'Keeffe Museum, 110
Geronimo (Apache leader), 51, *51*, 133, *133*
Ghost Ranch, *8*
ghost towns, 40, 50
Gila Cliff Dwellings National Monument, 113, *113*
Gila monsters, 21
Gila National Forest, 20–21
Gila trout, 21
Gila Wilderness, 15
Glorieta Pass, 49
Goddard, Robert, 58, *58*, 99
Goodacre, Glenna, 77
Gorman, R. C., 76, 133, *133*
governors, 34, 35, 36, 38, 45, *57*, 62–63, 80, 82, 84, 85–86, *85*, *86*, 89, *89*, 135
Grants, 105
grasslands, 14, 50
Great Depression, *57*, 58
Great Plains region, 13, 14–15
Guadalupe Mountains, 15
Gutierrez, Sid, 134

Hanna, William, 134
health care, 63
Hernández, Benigno, *57*
Highlands University, 71
Hillerman, Tony, *77*, 134, *134*
Hilton, Conrad, 101, *101*
Hilton Hotels Corporation, 101
Hispanics, *7*, 49, 50, 52, 55, *57*, 58, 59, 65, 69, *77*, 107, *107*
Hobbs, 115
hogans (Navajo homes), 30
Hohokam people, 25
Hopi people, 29
Houser, Allan, 76–77, 134
housing, 25, 30, 40, *42*, 43, *54*, 99
Hurd, Peter, 76

ice age, 23
Ice Cave, 105
illegal immigration, 62–63
immigrants, 52, 56, *57*, 59, 62, 70, 72
Indian Affairs Department, 89
Indian Pueblo Cultural Center, 107
Indian Wars, 51–52
insect life, 15
Intel corporation, 99
International UFO Museum, 114, *114*
interstate highways, *102*
Isotopes (baseball team), 78–79

jaguars, 21
Jefferson, Thomas, 41
jewelry, 74, *74*, *75*
jobs, 50, 52, 56, 57, 58, 61, 62, *62*, 65, 68, 92, 93, 95, 99
judicial branch of government, 83, 86–87, *87*

kachinas (Pueblo spirits), 30
Kiowa people, 51
Kirk, George H., *59*
Kit Carson Home and Museum, 109
kivas (underground rooms), 27, 28, *28*, 29, 104

labor unions, 56
Lamy, Jean Baptiste, *47*, 134
land area, 9, 11

Land of Pueblos (Lew Wallace), 52
languages, 7, 30, 34, 39, 59, 69, 70, 71, 72, *77*, 89, 107, 135
Larrazolo, Octaviano, *57*, 86, *86*
Las Cruces, 17, 66, *66*, 71, 112
Las Vegas, 71, 106
laws, 47, 68, 83, 84, 85, 86, 87
legislative branch of government, 82–83, 84–85, *84*, 86
Lincoln County War, 50
literature, 47, 70, 77–78, 133
livestock, 49, 50, 69, 93, 94, *94*
Living Desert Zoo and Gardens State Park, 115
Llano Estacado ("palisaded plain"), *13*, 14–15
The Lobos (sports teams), 79
"Long Walk," 51
López, George, 75, *75*
Lopez, Nancy, 79, *79*
López, Sabinita, *75*
Loretto Chapel, 110, *110*
Los Alamos, 60, 61, 71, 111
Los Alamos National Laboratory, 99, 111
Louisiana Purchase, 41, *41*
Luhan, Mabel Dodge, 134

magistrate courts, 86–87
Manhattan Project, 60
manufacturing, 57, 58, 92, 97, 100
maps
    agricultural, *97*
    counties, *88*
    European exploration, *37*
    interstate highways, *102*
    Louisiana Purchase, *41*
    mining, *97*
    national parks, *19*
    Native Americans, *26*
    New Mexico Territory, *53*
    New Spain colony, *34*
    population density, *67*
    Santa Fe, *83*
    statehood, *53*
    topographical, *10*
mariachi music, 77
marine life, 20, 21
Martínez, Antonio José, 134

Martinez, Esther, 134
Martinez, Julian, 74
Martinez, Maria, 74, *74*, *134*
McJunkin, George, 25, *25*
McKitrick, Jordan, 81
Mendoza, Don Antonio de, 34
mesas, 14, 20
Metropolitan Courthouse, *87*
Mexican Americans, 7, 50, 52, 57, 59, 65, 69, 107, *107*
Mexican free-tailed bats, 15
Mexican gray wolves, 21, *21*
Mexican spotted owls, 21, *21*
Mexican War, 45–46, *45*
Mexica people, 7
Mexico, 41, 45, 46, 82
military, 59, *59*, 60, *60*, 62, 63, *63*, 81, 99
Mimbres people, 25
Mineral Hot Springs, 113, *113*
mining, 41, 50, 56, 59, 93, 97, *97*, 98–99
Mogollon-Datil region, 13, 15
Mogollon people, 25, 113
molybdenum mining, 99
Momaday, N. Scott, 70, *70*
municipal courts, 86
Museum Hill, 110–111
Museum of Indian Arts and Culture, 111
Museum of International Folk Art, 110
Museum of Natural History and Science, 107, *107*
Museum of Spanish Colonial Art, 111
museums, 83, 106, 107, *107*, 109, 110–111, 111, 112, 114, *114*, 115
music, *77*, 77

Nageezi, 104
Nakayama, Roy, 96, *96*
national forests, 20
National Hispanic Cultural Center, 107, *107*
national parks, 15, 16, *19*, 115, *115*
"nations," 68, 89
Native American All-Star Game, 78–79

Native Americans, *7*, 23, 24–25, *24*, *26*, 27–28, *27*, 29–30, 30–31, *31*, 34, 35, 36, 38–40, *39*, 42, 43, 45, 46–47, 48, 49, 50, 51–52, *51*, 59, *59*, 61, 62, 63, 65, 68, 69, *69*, 70, 71, 74–75, 76, 77, 78–79, 89, 96, 98, 101, *101*, 104, 105, *105*, 107, 108, 111, 113, 133, 134, 135
natural gas, 63, 86
Navajo Gallery, 133
Navajo language, 135
Navajo people, 30, 49, 51, 59, *59*, 63, 69, *69*, 75, 76, 98, 104, 115
New Deal, 58
Newman, Larry, 79
New Mexican Hispanic Culture Preservation League, 108
New Mexico Farm and Ranch Heritage Museum, 112
New Mexico Institute of Mining and Technology, 71
New Mexico Museum of Space History, 114
New Mexico State Fair, 64
New Mexico State University, 71, 79, 96, 112
New Mexico Territory, 45–46, *53*
New Spain colony, 34, *34*, 82
Niza, Marcos de, 34–35, 135
NuMex Big Jim chile pepper, 96

oil, *62*, 63, 86, 93, 98–99
O'Keeffe, Georgia, 76, *76*, 110, 134
Old Fort Sumner Museum, 115
Old Town, 40
Olvera, Isabel de, 36
Oñate, Juan de, 35–36, 38, 89, 135
Oppenheimer, J. Robert, 60, 135
Ortega, Katherine, 135, *135*
Ortiz, Alfonso, 30, *30*
Otero Mesa, 20
Otero-Warren, Adelina "Nina," 57, *57*

Palace of the Governors, 38, *38*, 52, 83, 110, *110*
palisades, 13–14

Pecos, 112
Pecos National Historical Park, 112
Pecos River, 14, *14*
Peralta, Pedro de, 38
Petroglyph National Monument, 22, 108
petroglyphs, 36
piñon nuts, 18, 73, *73*, 96
piñon (state tree), 18
pistachio nuts, 96
pit houses, 25
plant life, 11, 18–19, *18*, 21, 25, 115
Polk, James, 45
Popé (Pueblo leader), 39, 40, 135
population, 47, 52, 55, 61, 65, 66, 67, 68, 70
posole (stew), 73
potash, 98
pottery, 25, 29, *29*, 74–75, *105*
pronghorn antelope, 20, *20*
Pueblo Bonito, 28, *28*, 104
Pueblo people, 29, 30, 31, *31*, 36, 38–40, 42, 45, 52, 55, 69, 74, 79, *101*, 107, 108, 133, 134, 135
Pueblo Revolt, 38–40
pueblos, 27, 28, *28*, 29, 45, 68, *74*, 89, 101, 104, 109, *109*
Pyle, Ernie, 135

radiation, 98
railroads, 50, 52, 56, 61, 70, 109
Ramah, 105
ranching, 50, 94, *94*
recipe, 73
Red Bluff Reservoir, 9, 11
Red Chile Sauce recipe, 73
referendums, 85
religion, 27, 28, 29–30, 35, 38–39, 40, 46, *46*, 47, 75
reptilian life, 20
Resa, Juan Guerra de, 36
reservations, 49, 51, 62, 63, 68, 70, 89, 101, 115
Richardson, Bill, 62–63, *80*, 85, *85*
Rio Grande, 11, 12, 14, 15, 19, 29, 36, 40
Rio Grande Rift, 12, *12*, 13, 15
Rio Rancho, 66

roadrunner (state bird), 20
roadways, 28, 61, *102*
rock carvings, 108
Rocky Mountains, 13, 15
Roman Catholicism, 46, *46*, *47*, 71
Roosevelt, Franklin D., 58
Roosevelt, Teddy, 52, 106
Roswell, 66, 114
Roswell Army Air Field, *63*
Rough Rider Memorial Collection, 106
Rough Riders, 52, 106
Roundhouse (state capitol), 82, 82, 83, 111
rural areas, 66–67

Sacramento mountain range, 16
San Andres mountain range, 16
Sandia National Laboratory, 60, 61, 99
Sandia Peak, 108, *108*
Sangre de Cristo Mountains, 15
San Ildefonso, 75
San Miguel Mission, *46*
Santa Fe, 35, 36, 38, *38*, 40, *41*, *44*, *45*, 46, 49, 52, 66, 71, 77, 82, *82*, 83, *83*, *88*, 92, 110–111
Santa Fe Trail, 44, 47, 49
Santa Rosa, 106
santeros (santo artists), *75*
Santillanes, Millie, 108
Santo Domingo Pueblo, *74*
Sawape pueblo, 27
sculpture, *76–77*
Seismosaurus (dinosaur), 12
service industries, 100, 101–102
settlers, 35–36, 38, 39–40, *39*, *41*, 43, 44–45, *44*, 47, 50, 51, 52, 69, 75, 135
Seven Cities of Gold. *See* Cíbola.
Shidoni foundry, *92*
Shiprock, 104, *104*
Shirley, Joseph, 98
Silver City, 50, 113
silver mining, 41, 98
Sky City, 105

slavery, 44–45, 47–48, 49
Socorro, 50, 71, 112
Sonoran desert, 15
sopaipilla (food), *73*
space flight, 99, 134
Spaceport America, 100
space travel, 100
Spanish exploration, 7, *32*, 33, 133
Spanish language, 107
Spanish settlers, 35–36, 38, 39–40, *39*, 43, 52, 69, 75
sports, 78–79, 136, *136*
state bird, 20
state capital, 82, 83, *83*, *88*
state capitol, *38*, *80*, 82, *82*, 83, 111
state constitution, 87
state flag, 83, 90, *90*
state fossil, 11
state grass, 14
statehood, 45, 47, 52, 55
state motto, 91
state name, 7
state nickname, 9
state parks, 58
state question, 72
state seal, 91, *91*
state tree, 18
St. John's College, 71
supreme court, 86, 87

Taos, 17, 43, 45, 61, 68, 71, 74, 76, 109, *109*, 134
Taos Pueblo, 45, 68, 109, *109*
Taos Ski Valley, 109, *109*
Tapahonso, Luci, 77, 135, *135*
technology industries, 62, 93, 99
Tewa language, 89
topographical map, *10*
tourism, 50, 61, *61*, 101, 108
transportation, 50
Trinity test site, 60
Trujillo, Miguel, 62, *62*
Truth or Consequences, 113
Tucumcari, *61*
Tularosa Basin, 16
Tularosa Fiesta, *78*
Turner, Ted, 106

University of New Mexico, 71, *71*, *79*, 99, 133
Unser, Al, 79, 136
Unser, Al, Jr., 79, 136, *136*
Unser, Bobby, 79
Upham, 100
uranium mining, 98
Urlacher, Brian, 79, 136, *136*

Valencia, 71
Vargas, Don Diego de, 40, 136
Vermejo Park Ranch, 106
Very Large Array, 99, 112, *112*
Villa, Pancho, 56, *56*
volcanoes, 12, 15, 17, 103, 105, 106, 107

Wallace, Lew, 52
Wallace, Susan, 52, *52*
water, 86
Wauneka, Annie Dodge, 63, *63*
weaving, *75*, *75*
Web sites, 16, 25, 30, 49, 50, 52, 57, 58, 62, 63, 70, 74, 75, 76, 79, 85, 86, 89, 96, 100, 101, 108
Western Heritage Museum, 115
Wheeler Peak, 9, 11, 15
Wheelwright Museum of the American Indian, 111
White, Jim, 16, *16*
White Sands Missile Range, 60, 99
White Sands National Monument, 16, *16*, 114, *114*
wildlife. *See* animal life; insect life; marine life; plant life; reptilian life.
Williams, Cathay, 48, 136
Willman, Cheryl, 100, *100*
Wilson, Heather, 136
World War II, 58–60, *59*

Zia people, 90
Zuni, 104
Zuni people, 29
Zuni Pueblo, 104

AUTHOR'S TIPS AND SOURCE NOTES

★ ★ ★

Ever since I first learned about the Taos Pueblo, I've been fascinated with the people and places of New Mexico. Since 1996, I've taken three trips there. The most recent one was in 2006, to do research for this book.

A number of books and Web sites helped expand my knowledge of New Mexico's history and culture. To learn more about the Pueblos, Navajos, and Apaches, as well as the Anasazis who came before them, I consulted Raymond Friday Locke's *The Book of the Navajo* and David E. Stuart's *Anasazi America*. Also helpful were Alvin M. Josephy's *500 Nations* and the various tribes' and pueblos' Web sites.

For general New Mexico history, I read several books by Marc Simmons of the University of New Mexico. The most helpful was *New Mexico: An Interpretative History*. For more recent events, I relied on *New Mexico: Past and Future*, by Thomas E. Chávez, and *Larger Than Life: New Mexico in the Twentieth Century*, by Ferenc M. Szasz. A useful book for learning more about sites I haven't visited yet was Nancy Harbert's *New Mexico*. Online editions of two of the state's major newspapers, the *Albuquerque Journal* and the *Santa Fe New Mexican*, kept me informed on the latest news.